FILM STUDIES

THE BASICS

Whether it's *The Matrix* or *A Fistful of Dollars* that's brought you
to film studies, this is a lively and thorough introduction to exactly
what you will be studying during your course.

Film Studies: The Basics will tell you all you need to know about:

- the movie industry, from Hollywood to Bollywood;
- who does what on a film set;
- the history, the technology and the art of cinema;
- theories of stardom, genre and film-making.

Including illustrations and examples from an international range of
films drawn from over a century of movie making and a glossary of
terms for ease of reference, *Film Studies: The Basics* is a must-have
guide for any film student or fan.

Amy Villarejo won the 2005 Katherine Singer Kovacs Book Award
from the Society for Cinema and Media Studies for her book
Lesbian Rule: Cultural Criticism and the Value of Desire. She is
Associate Professor in Film at Cornell University, USA.

ALSO AVAILABLE FROM ROUTLEDGE

FILM STUDIES
THE BASICS

Amy Villarejo

Routledge
Taylor & Francis Group

LONDON AND NEW YORK

First published 2007
by Routledge
2 Park Square, Milton Park, Abingdon, Oxon, OX14 4RN

Simultaneously published in the USA and Canada
by Routledge
270 Madison Ave, New York, NY 10016

Routledge is an imprint of the Taylor & Francis Group, an informa business

© 2007 Amy Villarejo

Typeset in Aldus Roman and ScalaSans by
Taylor & Francis Books
Printed and bound in Great Britain by
TJ International Ltd, Padstow, Cornwall

British Library Cataloguing in Publication Data
A catalogue record for this book is available from the British Library

Library of Congress Cataloging in Publication Data
A catalog record for this book has been requested

ISBN10: 0-415-36138-9   ISBN13: 978-0-415-36138-5 (hbk)
ISBN10: 0-415-36139-7   ISBN13: 978-0-415-36139-2 (pbk)
ISBN10: 0-203-01203-8   ISBN13: 978-0-203-01203-1 (ebk)

CONTENTS

LIST OF FIGURES

LIST OF BOXES

INTRODUCTION TO FILM STUDIES

If you've picked up this book to learn something about what it means to study film, you already know in large measure what cinema is: you've been watching movies since you first toddled out to the family television set, or since you braved your first excursion to a multiplex matinee. If you're old enough, you may have witnessed formats come and go. Perhaps you thrilled in your first chance to watch a beloved film at home on video, rewinding the tape over and again to watch Gene Kelly singin' in the rain or Greta Garbo unleashing her famous first spoken line in *Anna Christie* (Jacques Feyder, 1931): "Gimme a whiskey, ginger ale on the side, and don't be stingy, baby." DVDs, now repackaged with all of the "extras" that persuade us to replace those VHS tapes, may soon go the way of CDs, consigned right into the dustbin that receives the detritus of digital culture. Who knows? You may be born into a world in which cinema streams in bits onto our computer screens more than it lights up the screens of our neighborhood theaters.

No matter your point of entry into the matrix, welcome. Cinema lives and has always lived in multiple forms, some slowly dying, some newly emerging. In the late nineteenth century, cinema itself emerged from a diverse world of toys and machines that created the illusion of movement. Christened with perversely scientific names, these Phenakistoscopes, Thaumatropes, Zoetropes, and Praxinoscopes (all versions of spinning motion toys) competed with magic lantern projections and panoramas to entertain audiences with dizzying perspectives and steaming locomotives, acrobatic feats and elaborate stories. Forms of magic lanterns collected at the George Eastman House in Rochester (Lampascopes, Kodiopticons, Moviegraphs, and even a contraption dubbed "Le Galerie Gothique") testify to the ingenuity and variety of "pre-cinema." Some project, throwing larger-than-life images from slides onto screens and surfaces. Others invite spectators into more private viewings, into simulacra of theaters or, as with the later Edison Kinetoscopes, into solitary "peep" shows of sequential images that suggest movement. Some exploit the ideas of sequence or series, while others concentrate on the fantastic and imaginary worlds of storytelling. Taken as a whole, they anticipate but don't quite cross the threshold of cinema's illusion of continuous movement.

Enter early photographic studies of motion. Eadweard Muybridge perfected the large-scale photographic panorama of San Francisco in 1878, a sequence of thirteen photographs taken at different moments that together offer the spectator a 360° view of the city from atop Nob Hill. As opposed to the painted panorama, which conceals or renders irrelevant issues of duration, the photographic series creates from many individual instants an illusion of continuity: "many hours of the day masquerading as a single supreme moment, like a film in which segments shot at various times are edited into a believable narrative" (Solnit 2003: 176). But it is Muybridge's later famous analysis of a trotting horse that transforms those possibilities for thinking about time and motion that led to cinema's creation. The story goes like this: California former governor, robber baron, and racing horse aficionado Leland Stanford wanted to know whether, in the course of a trotting horse's stride, all four hooves were ever off the ground at once, and he hired California's best photographer (though he was both an Englishman and a murderer – no causal relationship implied) to find out. Muybridge's feat was not only to string threads across the race track to be tripped by the trotting horse, each triggering a camera's shutter in turn, but actually to create images from these enormously quick exposures. Silhouettes of the horse, to give him his due named Occident, answered affirmatively to Stanford's question, but the larger accomplishments, practical and philosophical, are his legacy (see Figure 1.1). First, Muybridge had to create what was in essence a film studio at the racetrack; to compensate for slow film speeds, he created a blindingly white environment for the horses to pass through, complete with distance markers and choice framings. Second, Muybridge fused technological development (of the triggers, shutters, chemistry) with the subjects he sought to photograph in order to invent a new medium, much as the cinema was to do in the decade following Muybridge's study for Stanford. But, third, Muybridge returned movement, and movement in a series that anticipates narrative, to photography:

> Muybridge had reduced the narrative to its most basic element: the unfolding of motions in time and space. Most of his sequences depicted the events of a few seconds or less, and he boasted that the individual exposures were as brief as one two-thousandth of a second. By imposing stillness on its subjects, photography had represented the world as a world of objects. But now, in Muybridge's work, it was a world of

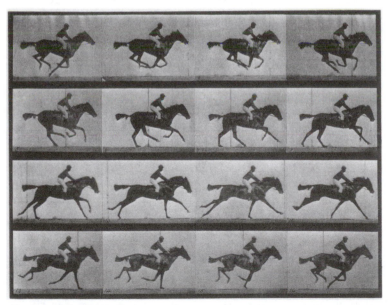

Figure 1.1: Eadweard Muybridge.
Source: The Kobal Collection.

processes again, for one picture showed a horse, but six pictures showed an act, a motion, an event. The subject of the pictures was not the images per se but the change from one to another, the change that represented time and motion more vividly, more urgently, than the slow motion of parades passing and buildings rising. It was a fundamental change in the nature of photography and of what could be represented.

(Solnit 2003: 194)

Muybridge was not alone in this exploration, but it was his work, alongside the "chronophotographic" camera of French photographer Etienne-Jules Marey, that suggested a way of thinking about time and motion through successive **frames**. Cameras equipped with a **shutter**, creating an interval of blackness in the exposure of each frame of film coated with a light-sensitive **emulsion**, recorded frame after frame (from ten to forty frames per second, or **fps**) of whatever lay before it; when projected, again with a shutter moving and at the same rate, the human eye perceives the individual frames as continuous motion, due to a still-baffling phenomenon scientists first called "**persistence of vision**" and tend now to call "persistent afterimages." The cinema, then, arises truly from an interface: a technology of continuously moving still images and a process of perception on the part of the human spectator which readies him or her to receive this continuity as motion itself.

Thomas Edison's Kinetograph and the Cinématographe of the Lumière brothers in France soon recorded our first films upon the principles and techniques Muybridge made concrete: more acrobats and strongmen, like the stock images of the "pre-cinema," but also everyday images (the Lumière *actualités* of workers and babies) (see Figure 1.2). It was in the very interval between meeting Muybridge and meeting Marey, in fact, that Edison transferred his model for sound recording and playback to images:

He assigned the job of studying two apparatuses – one for the recording of images, baptized the Kinetograph, and the other for viewing them, named the Kinetoscope – to an employee with a passion for photography, the Englishman William Kennedy Laurie Dickson. The two men proceeded cautiously. Arriving in Paris for the Universal Exposition of 1889, Edison met Marey, who told him about the progress of his own work. Eventually, in order to record photographic views, the American

Figure 1.2: Lumière Brothers.
Source: The Kobal Collection.

inventor abandoned the cylinder for a celluloid roll with perforations (sprocket holes) along each side, through which a toothed sprocket wheel would run; this ensured a uniform feed.

(Toulet 1995: 35)

To feed his Kinetoscopes, machines for peep show or solitary viewing, Edison built a movie studio in what were then the wilds of New Jersey, dubbed the "Black Maria" for its resemblance to the New York paddy wagons called by that name. From here Edison "cranked out" (a phrase derived from the hand-cranking of the camera) film after film: "Horses jumping over hurdles, Niagara Falls with its torrents plunging to rocky depths, trains rushing headlong across the screen, cooch-girls dancing, vaudeville acrobats taking their falls with aplomb, parades, boats, and people hurrying or scurrying along," summarized an early historian (Jacobs 1967 [1939]: 4). In France the Lumière brothers went a step further, perfecting a device that could record *and* project: the Cinématographe. Building upon Edison's invention, the Lumières solved the remaining problem of how to ensure that the film advances at a uniform rate to resynthesize the recorded image. The solution came to Louis Lumière in a dream: "In one night, my brother invented the Cinématographe," recalled Auguste (Toulet 1995: 40). Audiences responded hungrily and immediately to those images of ourselves "hurrying and scurrying" captured by mobile cameras and projected larger than life.

In the mid-1890s, in these first few years of cinema's life, congealed the essence of what we now mean when we refer to cinema. Above all, cinema is dynamic. It animates the world around us; it transports us to worlds we imagine or know only through images. Muybridge's experiments revealed the very idea of the interval: the transformation or mutation of the object from one state to the next, the essence of change itself. The inventor who soon became one of Edison's chief cinematographers, our passionate employee Englishman Dickson, dreamt deliciously of cinema's reach as early as 1895, when he and his wife wrote its first history:

> No scene, however animated and extensive, but will eventually be within reproductive power. Martial evolutions, naval exercises, processions and countless kindred exhibitions will be recorded for the leisurely gratification of those who are debarred from attendance, or who desire to recall them. The invalid, the isolated country recluse, and the harassed business man can indulge in needed recreation, without undue expenditure, without fear of weather, without danger to raiment, elbows and toes, and without the sacrifice of health or important engagements. Not only our own resources but those of the entire world will be at our command, nay, we may even anticipate the time when sociable relations will be established between ourselves and the planetary system, and when the latest doings in Mars, Saturn and Venus will be recorded by enterprising kinetographic reporters.
>
> (Dickson and Dickson 2000 [1895]: 51)

This took until 2005, when the first "cinematographer" of the Mars Rover mission received an Emmy Award nomination.

At the same time that we dream of cinema's reach, most of our films are literally dying: **prints** and **negatives** decomposing or bursting into flame, fading or melting into illegibility. Paolo Cherchi Usai, senior curator of the Motion Picture Department at George Eastman House and one of the leading figures in film preservation, elaborates on the philosophical, aesthetic and political consequences of the proliferation of images in the current moment combined with the phenomenon of the ongoing death of cinema, which can result from physical and environmental factors:

> In addition to the factors which can prevent its coming into being (malfunction of the apparatus, inadequate processing of the negative or its accidental exposure to light, human interference of various kinds), there is the host of physical and chemical agents affecting the image carrier: scratches or tears on the print caused by the projecting machine or its operator, curling of the film base as a result of a too intense exposure to the light source, colour alterations arising out of the film stock itself, environmental variables such as temperature and humidity. As soon as it is deposited on a matrix, the digital image is subject to a similar destiny; its causes may be different, but the effects are the same. Chronicles [read by Cherchi Usai] also mention catastrophes and extraordinary events such as fires, wars, floods, and destructive interventions from the makers themselves or the people who finance their activities.
>
> (Cherchi Usai 2001: 13)

By his estimate, fully 80 percent of the films made during the silent era (until the mid-1920s) are lost (Cherchi Usai 2001: 122). In Cherchi Usai's view, loss pervades the film experience, too. It is a product of the physical reality of perception, in which we "watch" a black screen each time a shutter passes over the projector, in which we turn away from the image each time we blink (according to the level of humidity in the room), in which we may find ourselves distracted or bored, drawn into reveries other than those onscreen. This physicality of perception alerts us to the fact that each viewing of a film is an evanescent experience, archived in memory, consigned to the realm of the unseen. If preservationists reclaim some of what has been lost, they and we will never be able to assert full or final control over the visible world; we will only catch glimpses of it. Experimental filmmaker Bill Morrison's *Decasia* (2002) is composed entirely of decaying archival footage, recording this process of loss. Seeking out footage filmed on highly flammable nitrate stock, Morrison painstakingly transferred this compilation of fragile images and set them to an original symphonic score: ghostlike figures (camels, dervishes) emerge out of the scratches, discolorations, and static to haunt us briefly before they yield to the texture of the film's surface.

BOX 1.1: THE UNITED STATES' LIBRARY OF CONGRESS

One treasure trove remains the United States' Library of Congress, which houses a very large film collection and makes available online over 400 early films, including those photographed by Dickson for Edison, through its American Memory collection.

SOME SAMPLE FILMS

General Lee's procession, Havana / Thomas A. Edison, Inc. (1899): A magnificent view of the Prado, from the balcony of the United States Club. The procession is headed by a troop of horsemen. Prominent among them is General Lee. Then come the soldiers, file after file and company after company; filling the broad avenue from curb to curb and as far as the eye can reach with marching men. It is the Seventh Army Corps. Great crowds of people fill the sidewalks; and through the trees that line the promenade in the middle of the Prado, are seen carriages and vehicles following the parade. The crowning event of the Spanish-American war! The great procession on Evacuation Day.

The boxing cats (Prof. Welton's) / Thomas A. Edison, Inc.(1894); producer, W.K.L. Dickson. A very interesting and amusing subject.

Edison kinetoscopic record of a sneeze, (January 7, 1894) / W.K.L. Dickson. Film made for publicity purposes, as a series of still photographs to accompany an article in *Harper's weekly*.

These films can be accessed through the Library of Congress website: www.loc.gov.

From its birth, then, until the present moment, cinema has assumed multiple guises and forms, circling into and out of sight, from its roots in the early motion of toys and machines: vaudeville-style exhibition, the invention of the "talkies" (from the recording of sound on discs to accompany films to today's use of digital Dolby surround sound), various uses of color (from early cinema's hand-tinted frames to Technicolor and beyond), widescreen formats like Cinemascope and VistaVision, different film **gauges** (from 8mm for home movies to the theatrical standard of 35mm and IMAX films in 65mm), and various reproductive, transfer, and storage technologies. And from those early kisses, trains, and trips to the moon? We may have replaced May Irwin, the first kissing lady of the screen, with J-Lo and "Bollywood babe" Udita Goswami, but we're still traveling.

WHY STUDY FILM?

Cinema's dynamism, its capacity to arrange and rearrange time and motion, thus reveals its dimensions that are deeply social, historical, industrial, technological, philosophical, political, aesthetic, psychological, personal, and so forth. The aggregate of these multiple dimensions indeed *is* cinema (for individual works I reserve the word "film" or "movie"). For enthusiasts, cinema rewards study like few other objects precisely because its reach is so great that it is never exhausted, its scope so varied that one rarely finds oneself thinking along a single plane of thought. Cinema is about everything and always about itself. About each image, we might ask, as Reynold Humphries does of the films of Jean-Luc Godard, "What values and ideas are already contained in an image from the fact of its mere presence?" (Humphries 1975: 13). If various images presented by cinema delight or thrill, agitate or unnerve, those images further offer themselves for analysis of their combinatory logic, for example. The great Soviet director Sergei Eisenstein, like the British (and later Hollywood) legend Alfred Hitchcock, advocated a science of audience stimulation whereby the director could calibrate, with unfailing precision, the image to the intended audience effect. While Eisenstein called his theory of combination **montage**, seeking to continue cinematically the political agitation of the Bolshevik Revolution, Hitchcock pursued his own ideas toward the end of pure response, what he among many others called "pure cinema," in the genre of the thriller:

Ernie, do you realize what we are doing in this picture? The audience is like a giant organ that you and I are playing. At one moment we play this note and get this reaction, and then we play that chord and they react that way. And someday we won't even have to make a movie – there'll be electrodes implanted in their brains, and we'll just press different buttons and they'll go 'oooh' and 'aaah' and we'll frighten them, and make them laugh. Won't that be wonderful?

(Spoto 1984: 440)

Likewise, if particular stories emerge from particular socio-historical contexts, those narratives benefit from careful study of their correspondences and divergences with the moment or context, but also of how they *mold* their moments and contexts, sometimes indelibly. Orson Welles' *Citizen Kane* (1941) both studies American isolationism in the first years of the Second World War *and* argues against it through the "fictional" figure of Charles Foster Kane, living a life of self-imposed isolation amidst the relics of memory, himself based upon newspaper and film magnate William Randolph Hearst. The extraordinary Senegalese filmmaker Ousmane Sembene both comments on the politics of foreign aid to African countries in one of his best films, *Guelwaar* (1992), *and* structures his critique of political violence, religious intolerance, and patriarchal authority around its murderous effects (see Figure 1.3).

The study of cinema, in other words, is emphatically not an attempt to arrest its dynamism, to still it in order to subject it to scrutiny. It is rather the pursuit of cinema as an historical hydra, with tentacles reaching into all aspects of our individual and collective lives. This book traces several of those tentacles in each of its five subsequent chapters. It is not meant to be a comprehensive introductory textbook but rather an engaging and provocative accompaniment to what is for most people a lifelong relationship with the cinema. Toward that end, *Film Studies: The Basics* offers the reader multiple ways in which to situate, to enrich, and to enlarge his / her knowledge and experience of film; it hopes to be a companion as well as a guidebook to adventurous and wondrous viewing.

Chapter 2 offers a quick primer in the language of film analysis or the formal study of film (covering **cinematography**, *mise-en-scène*, **editing**, sound, and narrative), demonstrating that some specialized terms are essential for understanding how films work

Figure 1.3: Ousmane Sembene.
Source: Films Terre Africaine, Les/The Kobal Collection.

and how films solicit our attention and responses. Some historical understanding of cinema is likewise crucial for understanding the medium today: how it not only reflects but shapes history. For the reader seeking a basic knowledge of the field of film studies, then, Chapters 2 and 3 essentially open up the arenas of film analysis and film history, both taught widely, if frequently separately, in many colleges and universities. Toward a second goal of offering a rudimentary introduction to further and more advanced intellectual issues and questions of film study, two chapters on production / exhibition and reception follow. These provide a more subjective assessment of the bread-and-butter issues of film studies as an academic discipline: the relation between art and industry, questions of genre and authorship, film censorship, film labor, technologies of cinema, exhibition histories and practices, stardom and fandom, publicity / marketing / promotion, spectatorship, film theories, and the like. The final chapter treats film in the context of emergent media and new academic configurations: digital culture, new media, visual studies. Together the chapters privilege the "why" of cinema study by surveying the "what" (substance), "when" (history), "who" (makers and viewers), and "how" (mechanisms) of film. My overarching goal is to offer the reader an exposure to the infectious enthusiasm, if not mania, that is cinephilia, while simultaneously providing a grounding in the study of cinema that will make future viewing more rewarding.

WHAT IS FILM?

If I've made reference to your experience as first-time popcorn munchers at the multiplex, or as DVD buyers or renters, it has been to enlist you in the conviction that you have already some considerable experience with a variety of different types of films. You are an expert already, with a feel for what you like and don't like: a sense, for example, of when American director Tim Burton's aesthetic vision seems exciting (*Edward Scissorhands*, 1990) or shallow (*Planet of the Apes*, 2001), or a marked (and deserved) preference for Jet Li over Jackie Chan. You find yourself so saturated with the conventions of genre (drum beats signaling threat in suspense films, crescendos of violin strings accompanying romantic unions in melodramas, stock characters in B-westerns, and predictable scenarios in horror spinoffs) that you spend hours delighting in their violations or spoofing on *The Simpsons* or through sophisticated generic revisions in French *noir*. You live amidst cinema, just as a student of economics lives within an economy. Cinema, however, is just as naturalized as is our economy; that is, its dominant rules, its habitual narratives, its general visual styles, its mode of production, its sites of exhibition, its **tie-ins** (product placements, ties to other commodities like Burger King cups or toy dolls), even its running times, tend to be taken as given, as natural, as unquestioned, and as unchanging. The first step, then, in film education is to notice what we take to be given, true, "how things are," in order that we may confirm, revise, or reject those same assumptions when tested against the most expansive understanding of and inquiry into cinema.

"FILMS TELL STORIES"

Many films do tell stories, thanks to the overwhelming dominance of commercial **narrative** (a chain of events in a cause–effect relationship) cinema. Not so for much of early cinema: its musclemen and magic tricks hewed more to what film historian Tom Gunning calls the "cinema of attractions." Aping theatrical presentations, these films settle the camera into the chair of a hypothetical audience member and train it upon a proscenium, upon which unfolds some daredevil feat or anomalous bodily act. In a portrait of contortionist virility, the amazing Sandow (Prussian Schwarzenegger-precursor Eugen Sandow) expands his chest from its normal forty-seven buff inches to an incredible sixty-one, and holds a platform of three horses, weighing about 3000 pounds, above his head. The goal? Extracting an unadulterated "awesome!" and nothing more. If virility is reserved for the likes of Sandow and Buffalo Bill, flexibility and plasticity characterize other immigrant groups: Chinese acrobats poke heads through crossed legs, while gun juggling and knife tumbling are done by "an illustrious Moor," Dickson tells us (Dickson and Dickson 2000 [1895]: 40). These early films, often a single **shot** long (a length of continuously exposed film), exploit the capacity of the cinema to *show*, to dazzle, to capture our attention. In the early years of cinema, Gunning reminds us, the cinema itself was the attraction, and it was linked as much to practices of storytelling as to the kinds of modern conceptions of time and space discovered in Muybridge's motion studies or in visual culture more largely. While narrative films emerged with the first decade of the cinema, then, and while they largely replaced these "attractions," elements of this cinema of attractions nonetheless persist in our day. With breathless enthusiasm and reverence for their technological accomplishments, we call them "special effects." (These, too, are the most frequent occasions for the question "How did they do that?," which we'll explore in Chapter 2.)

A second arena of film that is non-narrative we refer to as "experimental" or *avant-garde* cinema. A film, for example, called *The Flicker* (Tony Conrad, 1965) – a product of perhaps an excessive fondness in that decade for mind alteration and hallucinogens – alternates frames that are entirely white and entirely black for more than thirty minutes. The pulsating result, inducing anything from entrancement to nausea to rare epileptic seizures, inspired a wave of subsequent experimental makers to create non-narrative experiments in perception. Other experimental films reject narrative in favor of other forms of meaning-making, aesthetic effect, or perceptual experience, and many simultaneously reject the idea of recording a latent image from a prior reality. Artists such as Bruce Connor (in his brilliant film on apocalyptic time, *A Movie* [1958]) or, more recently, Craig Baldwin (in his compilation agitprop films, including *Spectres of the Spectrum* [2000]) use **stock** or **found footage** in order to explore the social consequences of technological innovation and to challenge complacency. The late Stan Brakhage, one of the monumental experimental filmmakers of the twentieth century, attached moth wings (and a few bodies and blades of grass) to film leader and ran it through a projector in *Mothlight* (1963); early *avant-garde* makers such as Man Ray (in his "Rayograms" from the 1920s and 1930s) placed objects directly on film stock and exposed it to light, much as children do today with paper clips, photographic paper, and sunshine.

"MOST FILMS COME FROM HOLLYWOOD"

Dubbed the "dream factory" in an early study by anthropologist Hortense Powdermaker, Hollywood has indeed become synonymous with the movies, and for good reason. American film, like other American commodities, floods the world's markets, whether due to discrepancies in copyright law, lack of funds directed toward national film industries or partnerships, the deregulation of markets, or globalized corporate structures. The largest film industry in the world is not, however, that of the United States. That distinction has for many years instead belonged to India, a country which produces 800 to 900 films per year, about a quarter of which, mainly Hindi superproductions involving huge stars and musical numbers, emerge from "Bollywood" (Bombay Hollywood), compared to dwindling numbers of productions in the United States. The regulation of American exports in countries such as China – the Chinese government's attempt to stimulate an indigenous industry – have not bred solutions, only further problems, such as widespread, overwhelming piracy of DVDs. While Anglophone audiences likely see Hong Kong action pictures or Japanese animation (called *anime*), few except city-dwellers with access to first-rate art or repertory theaters seek out "foreign" films in theatrical release, and their dearth contributes to the persistent impression that Hollywood cinema dominates onscreen.

Even the assumption, moreover, that films emanate from "national" industries requires upending, and not simply because we find ourselves in an increasingly "globalized" industry, as I shall discuss at further length in Chapter 3. National film industries have never been "pure," even when they have been most forcefully tied to the nation-state, such as when the German or Italian film industries were overtly harnessed to the Nazi and Fascist regimes during the Second World War. Italian cinema under Mussolini produced propaganda, yes, but it also produced scores of melodramas, comedies, and films of social interest involving some of the extraordinarily talented figures, such as Vittorio DeSica, we tend now to associate with the Italian post-war cinematic movement called "neorealism." Later, when the American studio system began to collapse as it competed with television and squandered enormous amounts of money on **blockbusters** (expensive and widely promoted superproductions), the Italian cinema yoked itself to units devoted to American "international" productions. "Spaghetti" westerns were born of the union. Many of those films, especially those directed by Sergio Leone and featuring scores by Ennio Morricone, have become the stuff of film-buff legend; the famous line delivered by James Coburn in *A Fistful of Dynamite* (1971) before spectacularly blowing up his enemies – "Duck, you sucker" – is an anthem of their style, a peculiar amalgam of brazen violence and camp wit. There's much more to these films than style, however: *Fistful*'s plot, centered around the mysterious entrance of an Irish Republican Army (IRA) explosive expert upon the scene of the Mexican Revolution, displays the extent to which ideas of America, that complicated promise of freedom amidst histories of social repression, circulate in fantastic spaces only movies can create. "Which way is America?" asks one of the film's characters, revealing a fusion of Europe and the Americas in which, as film scholar Marcia Landy observes, "most modern discourses of nation are unstable constructions" (Landy 1996: 69). Even "Hollywood" itself wobbles on its national foundation: from the works of émigré directors like Douglas Sirk (né Dietlef Sierck) and Fritz Lang to those of Paul Verhoeven (who directed *Basic Instinct* [1992]) and Jan de Bont (of *Speed* [1994] fame), the American cinema absorbs and cannibalizes, and is absorbed and cannibalized in turn by, the rest of the world.

"FILMS STAR, WELL, STARS"

(A different assumption from the more complicated, and certainly equally contestable, assertion that stars, well, act.)

Overwhelmed by the mega-salaries commanded by the likes of Julia Roberts and Tom Cruise, we may feel licensed to assume that the institution of stardom in Hollywood (1) is alive and well and (2) has deviated only slightly from the system found there during its heyday, when Mary Pickford and Douglas Fairbanks built their castle called "Pickfair" in the Hollywood Hills, or when the studio Metro-Goldwyn-Mayer (MGM) boasted "more stars than there are in heaven." The story of the emergence of modern stardom offers a palpable index of that institution's pliability and discontinuities: as much as we now attribute early films to their innovative directors (like Thomas Edison, or Edwin S. Porter, or, later, D.W. Griffith), most films before 1910 or thereabouts instead were advertised entirely as products of **studios** (those complex techno-industrial entities that organized film labor through most of the twentieth century). We owe the idea of the modern female star to Carl Laemmle. He was the head of the Independent Motion Picture (IMP) company who launched an innovative promotional campaign in 1910 for a player named Florence Lawrence, known previously only as "the Biograph girl." One morning, so the story goes, readers of the St. Louis (Missouri) newspapers learned of the death of their beloved "Biograph girl" Florence Lawrence (the first time her name had been used publicly) in an unfortunate streetcar accident. Immediately thereafter, Laemmle responded with a blasting notice that the story (which, it should not surprise you, he himself had planted) was a vicious lie: "Miss Lawrence was not even in a streetcar accident, is in the best of health, will continue to appear in 'Imp' films, and very shortly some of the best work in her career is to be released" (Jacobs 1967 [1939]: 87). He followed up the stories with a visit from Florence Lawrence and the IMP's leading man, King Baggott, to put all doubts to rest, and adoring crowds, delighted that Florence Lawrence was alive, received them.

If Laemmle created America's first star, and perhaps America's first star couple in Lawrence–Baggott, he also gave form to the couple that is more strongly cemented in this story of stardom's birth: the star and the promotion / publicity apparatus upon which he or she rests. For stars, as Robert Sklar notes in his wonderful history of cinema, are mysteries explained by no single variable: "beauty, performance style, or promotional effort" (Sklar 1993: 72). While they may function as intimates, surrogates, or (to use the language of psychoanalysis that many film scholars have brought to images of stars) "ego-ideals," stars can never be divorced from their screen *personae* and from the myths sustained about them by the industry and its parasites. Just as the cinema *is* the ensemble of its texts and their contexts, stardom is this fusion, and it includes the motor of our desire and pleasure. Stardom is, in other words, a social phenomenon, wherein stars can function as condensations for social anxieties, screens for desire, allegories for transgression, fictions for racial identities, tools for industrial profiteering, models for gender and sexual behavior, and so forth. Promotion and publicity can fuel stars' careers as much as they can destroy them: the greatest star of the silent Chinese (Shanghai) cinema, Ruan Ling-yu, committed suicide at the age of twenty-four, after a tabloid article focusing on her relationships with her estranged husband and lover compared her personal status to that of the "fallen women" she, like Greta Garbo, frequently played. Experimental filmmaker and author Kenneth Anger's chronicle of stars' demises, *Hollywood Babylon* (1975), exemplifies the other side of this kind of tragedy: the pleasure in dirt associated with the fall of stars from the heavens.

If stardom as institution has some historical and social specificity, it does not, however, extend over cinema in its entirety. With regard to narrative film, movements such as Italian neorealism, as well as those cinemas associated with struggles for national liberation (such as "Third Cinema"), feminist cinema, and queer cinema, all depend upon the use of non-professional actors to explore everyday life and the lives of the people constituted in these social and political collectivities. British director Mike Leigh's process combines non-professional with professional actors to inhabit the lives of his frequently working-class characters, which Leigh develops, largely unscripted, over the course of his films' production. Other processes rely upon the dynamics of ensemble casts of actors who know each other well and build improvisationally upon past work: the cycle of films directed by Christopher Guest (*Waiting for Guffman*, 1996; *Best in Show*, 2000; *A Mighty Wind*, 2003) could not provide better illustration of the hilarious fruits of this sort of collaboration. While a few documentary films may have created stars, such as Michael Moore's notoriety after documenting his pursuit of the General Motors chairman of the board in *Roger and Me* (1989), the practice of documentary tends to exploit stars mostly for their social authority; they can function as "talking heads" or provide "voice of God" narration (such as Morgan Freeman's in *March of the Penguins* [2005]) to convince audiences of a film's worth, thereby bolstering box office receipts. Finally, even those independent productions that have a strong narrative component frequently cannot afford stars whose names and reputations would bring them to distributors' and audiences' attention; many very fine projects founder in development purgatory, waiting for a star's interest, while just as many lousy ones careen through with green lights thanks to an agent's conviction.

"Films are in color." "Films last for about two hours." "Films are the products of directors' visions." "The best films receive Academy Awards." "The costs of films' production exceed the cost of their promotion." "Theater tickets generate movies' profit." "There are no great films from Poland (Mongolia, Ireland, Iran, Burkina Faso, . . .)." "Films are better now than they were fifty years ago." And so on: whatever your assumptions, film study encourages you to explode them, test them, examine them, compare them, historicize them. Make way, that is, for what you're seeing and hearing and learning, so that you can overcome the alienation factor that results from a film failing to conform to your expectations, however expansive. If you remain open to what a film might be, you are a step further toward thinking about what cinema will have been or might become.

WHAT IS CINEMA?

This question is one made famous, and unanswerably so, by the film theorist and *Ur*-cinephile André Bazin. A two-volume study of this title appeared in translation from the French in a 1971 paper-back edition; in the hands of students, the well-thumbed, slim pink and lime green volumes were indispensable signifiers of a serious and weighty interest not in films, still less in the movies, but in "The Cinema." The term meant at least the following: a vast knowledge of film history and its canon, a well-honed aesthetic sensibility, an attentiveness to films' formal language and structures, a political understanding of post-war consciousness and the forces condensed in the moment shorthanded as May 1968 in France, a passion for the philosophy of cinema (and / or cinema as philosophy), and a commitment to one or several eccentric critical gestures, such as taking the view (contrary to Bazin's and to every known Truth) that Buster Keaton was a greater physical comedian than Charlie Chaplin, say, or elevating a producer such as Pandro S. Berman (belatedly recognized by the 1977 Irving Thalberg Award from the Academy of Motion Picture Arts and Sciences) to an exalted status, a joke, but not only a joke, Gore Vidal plays out in his novel *Myra Breckenridge*. The Cinema combined a feel for the high and the low, balancing the weightiest questions about how to imagine human freedom with the feeling of frenetic delight in a Mack Sennett chase or the one following upon a funeral in the René Clair short film *Entr'acte* (1924). The Cinema, in the sense of Bazin's query, was not just a way of taking seriously something others dismissed as pabulum or "mere" entertainment (although it was that to be sure), but also a way of asking, more deeply than most before or after him, after the ontology, the essence, of cinema as it relates to our very being. How do certain approaches to life and to social being find cinematic expression? How does cinema help us approach the mystery of the human, the "real," that element of our existence toward which we incline only asymptotically, without ever fully apprehending it?

Bazin's writings, begun during the Second World War and extended through his short life until the 1950s, when he founded the French film magazine *Cahiers du cinéma*, have been read and re-read by generations of film students. His biographer, Dudley Andrew, is right in my view to see his impact as awe inspiring:

> André Bazin's impact on film art, as theorist and critic, is widely considered to be greater than that of any single director, actor, or producer in

this history of the cinema. He is credited with almost single-handedly establishing the study of film as an accepted intellectual pursuit.

(Bazin 1997: x)

In fact, Bazin was a kind of guru for those voracious students of cinema who became the leading directors of the French New Wave, such as Jean-Luc Godard and François Truffaut.

There is a danger, however, in simplifying his reflections on realism, which too readily become aligned with his fondness for the movement known as Italian neorealism, about which he wrote as it unfolded in Italy following the war, or his enthusiasm for the work of French director Jean Renoir (son of the Impressionist painter Pierre Auguste Renoir). In neorealism and in Renoir (but also in Orson Welles, William Wyler, and others), Bazin found something massive to push against, to test, to think about, which he called by the slippery and perhaps misleading name "realism." By this name, he referred to what is revealed by a style on a continuum at whose other pole is montage. At realism's end, the cinema is an art and practice of composition and contemplation; the director sets the image before the spectator, often through the long take (a shot of a relatively long duration) and **deep space** (the combination of deep focus, or maintaining many planes of action in focus simultaneously, with a set which allows the director to stage action on those many planes), whose active and curious gaze engages it and thereby finds it an avenue toward (not a "representation of") reality. Active, curious, intellectual, committed, open, fluid, engaged: these are the key words of this end of the continuum; but "realism," it must be stressed, does not designate its fulfillment in the "real," only a method for its approach, where "real" continues to stand for that kernel of the mystery of being we never access. At the other end of the continuum lies "montage," associated as we have seen with the work of Sergei Eisenstein in the (former) Soviet Union but also more generally with **classical Hollywood cinema** (explained at greater length in Chapter 2 and exemplified by D.W. Griffith, from whom Eisenstein learnt the rudiments of "analytical cutting"). Montage directs or restricts the viewer's attention through editing, limiting his / her capacity for contemplation, or for finding gaps or loose associations, by insisting upon meaning, supplying details, and otherwise didactically leading the way. As Bazin explains it in an essay on Wyler:

The technique of analytical cutting tends to destroy in particular the ambiguity inherent in reality. It "subjectivizes" the event to an extreme, since each shot is the product of the director's bias. Analytical cutting implies not only a dramatic, emotional, or moral choice, but also, and more significantly, a judgment on reality itself.

(Bazin 1997: 8)

The problems with the extremes of the continuum become immediately clear, insofar that positioning any given film or filmmaker on this spectrum would lead to a judgment about the director's political / philosophical value: Rossellini (one of the giants of neorealism) good, Hitchcock bad. Or, more perniciously, Rossellini politically progressive *due to his cinematic style*, and Hitchcock politically retrogressive *due to his*. But the kernel of Bazin's insights into the philosophical and political (and social, historical, industrial, technological, aesthetic, psychological, personal – and I need to add here "religious") nature of cinematic expression, how it is able to or unable to seize our collective interest and help it coalesce into deep insight about what one grandly used to call the human condition, should not be lost in continued questions about what cinema *is*. While located quite specifically in the years and works of the post-war period, Bazin's thinking inaugurated an inquiry in the cinema as equal to, and perhaps greater than (given its social power), any serious intellectual and political project.

If Bazin wasn't always quick to complicate his own dichotomizing scheme, his students later continued to follow its strict logic, but with new objects at hand. The contributors to *Cahiers*, avid cinephiles who gorged themselves on American films at the Cinémathèque française as soon as the French government lifted bans on their import following the war, turned attention in the 1950s to those directors who they believed managed to express themselves despite the assembly-line nature of industrial filmmaking. Carrying the seed of Bazin's valuation of agonistic, dialectical approaches toward the ever-elusive "real," they found in the style of some Hollywood genre films a cinematic vision that cut against the grain of standardization, conformity, and routine or rote production. They elevated these directors to the status of authors, or *auteurs* in French, as opposed to those "hacks" (or *metteurs en scène* in French) who were seen merely to be grinding out the already known. *Auteurs* found ways to "sign" their films, or, perhaps more accurately, the *Cahiers* writers found evidence for the Hollywood directors' signatures across bodies of their work, whether through attention to formal **motifs** (particularly those expressed through *mise-en-scène*, in the placement and movement of actors and objects within the frame), or, less frequently, through thematic preoccupations which nonetheless emerge from film style. When American film critics seized upon the French conception of film authorship, or the *politique des auteurs* (the notion that the director is ultimately able to express his – and it was uniformly gendered male – vision through the creative army at his disposal), they did so with a vengeance for taxonomy and hierarchy that dispensed with the care the *Cahiers* critics took to value the contributions of Hollywood to cinema more broadly understood. That is, the *Cahiers* contributors found art when they looked at Hollywood, art as valuable, "signed," and complex as the art cinema that emerged from Europe, Japan, India and elsewhere in the 1950s from director luminaries such as Ingmar Bergman, Federico Fellini, Satyajit Ray, Michelangelo Antonioni, Luchino Visconti, Andrei Wajda, Akiro Kurosawa, Yasujiro Ozu, Robert Bresson, Jacques Tati, and so on. And the struggle with the constraints of industrial production only upped the ante; whereas "art cinema" directors enjoyed total freedom and control, by comparison Hollywood directors labored under the boss they all called the Bottom Line. A western like *Stagecoach* (1939) or the later and far more folksy and racist epic *The Searchers* (1956) deserved close analysis and attention, then, for the director's capacity to make style speak through the tried and true formulae and conventions of classical cinema, thereby elevating John Ford to the *Cahiers* inner circle. And Ford especially, since he was the man who was so identified with genre films that when he introduced himself to Cecil B. DeMille (on the occasion of defending fellow director Joseph Mankiewicz against McCarthy-era charges of Communist sympathizing) he merely said, "My name's John Ford. I make Westerns" (Buscombe 1988: 344).

The legacy of the *Cahiers* writings is greater than some acknowledge, for that group insisted in important ways upon the value of commercial cinema, if only some of it, as meaningful and worthy of careful analysis for its contributions to an expressive repertoire and form of collective life. If the tendency of later critical assessments of the *politique des auteurs* has been understandably to bristle at the dichotomizing and dismissive hierarchies of "author / hack," "trash / art," "style / genre" that emerge from these analyses, those who engage with the popular commercial cinema as an object of study nonetheless owe some debt to Bazin and to their writings. It should not surprise us that Truffaut and Godard, like Quentin Tarantino a few decades later, gobbled up as much generic fare as possible, only to adopt it, transmute it, adapt it, revise it toward their own ends in the New Wave, for that group of filmmakers were as interested in Bazin was in a cinema of thought. Indeed, French theorist Gilles Deleuze finds in Godard something akin to Romanticism: "grasping the intolerable or unbearable, the empire of poverty, and thereby becoming visionary, to produce a means of knowledge and action out of pure vision" (Deleuze 1989: 18).

What is cinema, then, if not an opportunity for thought? To discover principles of form, to trace something of its history, to grasp its power to transform: these are the subjects of the following chapters.

BOX 1.2: SUMMARY

From its inception in the late nineteenth century, film has been a dynamic medium, put to uses other than those of the commercial narrative form. "The Cinema" designates the ensemble of films as they engage with the world of spectators, as we, in other words, respond in the broadest possible sense to what we see and hear. To study film, then, is to test our assumptions about what we take films to be, about what we might expect to see and hear, and to take films seriously as revealing something, again in the broadest possible sense, about who we have been, who we are, and who we might become. Commercial fare, like *Dude, Where's My Car* (2000), and radical documentary, like *This is What Democracy Looks Like* (from the same year and available to stream online), belong to the cinema, all of which opens itself to study.

THE LANGUAGE OF FILM

Film is structured like a language. Or is it? Composed of fundamental units, called shots, films rely upon **edits** to join shots
together into larger strings called **sequences** (a series of shots united
in time and space), just as words become sentences. Many films
depend for their intelligibility upon rules or cinematic **conventions**,
a form of film grammar that has evolved over time. A military
parade, such as the masses in motion in the German propaganda
film *Triumph des Willens / Triumph of the Will* (Leni Riefenstahl,
1935), always moves in the same onscreen direction, for example;
flashbacks, or **temporal ellipses** of many sorts, are often signaled
with a **dissolve** (that edit which joins two shots, the first fading
while the second gradually appears). And, like a language, new
elements, born of both technological innovation and imaginative
invention, enter the cinematic lexicon, while others disappear or
become anachronistic. Special effects master Dennis Muren's
compositing (mixing several visual components in one shot), as
Hollywood insider Anne Thompson notes, "makes possible the
morphing T-1000 in *Terminator 2* (1991) and the fleet-footed
dinosaurs in *Jurassic Park* (1993)" (A. Thompson 2005: 2). The use
of the **iris** (another edit, a round mask that closes to black, or that

opens to begin a sequence, or that encircles an important detail) has even come in recent years to signify "old-fashioned," associated as it is with the silent narrative cinema and with its trademark use in the Looney Tunes. Like language, film opens to different uses or forms. Some films are like stories, others more like novels or serials. Some films seem poetic; others, striving perhaps toward profundity, seem simply nonsensical. Some documentary films want their language to seem transparent, as much of the language of journalism aspires to be, while other films want us to do nothing more than to notice their language, as with filmic explorations of the *avant-garde* and other experimental makers.

The comparison *to* language beloved of some introductory courses in cinema, however, faces serious limits, demonstrated by film theorists over several decades. First, insofar as films involve **screen duration**: they cut out and rearrange time as they unfold in time (and as they unfold in time, in whatever format, remember that they are also dying). Films enlist our sensations, perceptions, and responses in and over time, as much as they appeal to our memories, our archives of what we know and have known, of what we experience and have experienced. They appeal to and become part of our personal and individual histories, and part of our collective lives. They also appeal to our linguistic being, such that what we might attribute to a film experience may in fact originate in our linguistic habits and expectations. I may experience the break-up of my relationship in the terms of melodrama, hurling lines such as "You never loved me!" in imitation of the best melodrama queens like Joan Crawford and Bette Davis; you show your friends the testimony in Claude Lanzmann's *Shoah* (1985) to convince them that the slogan of "never again" (will Jews suffer genocide) is complicated by collective loss experienced variably and individually. Only by making appeals to the way we move through the world, literally our "common sense," does the cinema endure, and only by doing so can cinema *rearrange* those unquestioned ideas, our unexamined relationships to the past, to history. Some films are notable for the way they dislocate time, fragment it, or interrupt its seemingly linear flow: Alain Resnais' films *Nuit et brouillard / Night and Fog* (1955) and *Hiroshima, mon amour* (1959) crucially contest our understandings of the monumental and personal devastations wrought by the Second World War, in the death camps and in the bombing of Hiroshima, respectively. But other films also play with history, if in more conventional ways, in order to challenge pious or commonsensical attitudes toward simple ways of understanding the past. *Bill and Ted's Excellent Adventure* (Stephen Herek, 1989) gives history over to the little guys, California high-school students who think Caesar is a salad dressing; while *The Watermelon Woman* (Cheryl Dunye, 1996) invents Hollywood history from the perspective of a black lesbian who is searching both for love and for (nonexistent) images of herself in the world of cinema.

Second, cinema's reach is everywhere; its time is its entire past. I suggested in Chapter 1 that if film preservationists were to deposit a fraction of what the cinema has been into an archive, that collection can never represent, as a portion of a dictionary does, a fraction of the elements available for the cinema's future. Cinema, in other words, bears a distinctly different relationship than does language to conceptions of totality: that's part of what makes it daunting (for one can never imagine, much less see, even a smidgen of what has been recorded) but also what makes it powerful, compelling, fascinating. For it bridges a gap between the self and the limitless whole, between what we know intimately and what we can never know. In an oscillation between innovation and industrial co-optation, between invention and repetition, cinema makes itself part of us, literally imprinting itself upon our retinas and lingering there. But also figuratively: we *speak* in the language of cinema, calling celebrity photographers "paparazzi" after the character of Paparazzo in Federico Fellini's *La Dolce Vita* (1960), or challenging an opponent with the line Clint Eastwood popularized in the Dirty Harry films: "Go ahead. Make my day." We *remember* in the language of cinema, summoning our images of Hitler, of John F. Kennedy, of the first space walk, or of true love from its vast archive. We *feel* through the language of cinema, in the bone-chilling effects of the thriller or in the deluges we unleash in the "weepies." Even through these intimate experiences of the cinema, however, we will still never really know what it has been or what it might become; its totality, as our own does, eludes us.

Finally, in understanding the comparison with language to obtain between scholarly approaches to film form and linguistic treatments of grammar – so that we are comparing the study of elements of film form and their rules of combination (shot, sequence, continuity editing or challenges thereto) with the study of elements of a given language and its rules (words, sentences, "correct" vs. "incorrect" usage) – we risk diminishing both film study and our conception of language and its study. We reduce both, in other words, to *normative* analyses, for to study a system and its rules is to reduce a phenomenon in order to make it manageable. Grammar elides other fascinating realms of linguistics: history, texts (philology), comparative linguistics, the philosophy of language, the study of its use, and the like. Film analysis – the name for the study of film as "like a language" through a taxonomy of its form and an examination of its rules – similarly brackets film history, theory, the philosophy of the image, fandom, technological shifts, industrial organization, and so on. Film analysis, furthermore, lends itself most powerfully to the study of narrative film, a dominant form, to be sure, but, as we have seen, by no means the only one.

As the words in bold throughout this book indicate, however, I find some specialized language nonetheless helpful for describing what we see and hear and then thinking deeply about it, just as the ability, I believe, to parse a sentence renders one's own writing more precise and nuanced in order to make an argument. Here in this chapter, then, I condense key areas of film analysis; in the remainder of the book, I visit some of these other ways of thinking through the phenomenon of cinema. The title of this chapter, "The language of film," means, then, to suggest that one learn the language of film analysis precisely in order to say something meaningful about a given film, or about cinema. After reading this chapter, you ought, for example, to be able to identify and describe (and these are all defined subsequently) **rear projection**, the **axis of action**, or a **tracking motif**. The point, however, and to paraphrase Karl Marx, is not simply to *describe* the world you see onscreen; it is to risk having a point in the description. The selection of key terms aims not to offer encyclopedic knowledge or the upper hand in trivia games, but instead to help you begin to think through different issues or questions that various formal strategies present. The question that ought to underlie close analysis, to put it bluntly, is "so what?" What is the function of x or y? What results from the choice of y over x? Why does x leave me cold? Or why does y convince me?

A note for future study: many fine textbooks extend the discussion of film analysis you are about to read. Two of them upon which many academics and college / university courses rely regularly are David Bordwell and Kristin Thompson, *Film Art: An Introduction* (1993), and Timothy Corrigan and Patricia White, *The Film Experience* (2004). Both texts multiply the number of terms I present here, and both acknowledge the paradoxical, if not impossible, nature of any taxonomy of film. In giving names to what we see and hear, that is, we necessarily translate; we represent, in the medium of written language, the sensory experience of watching and listening. (The still images sprinkled throughout this text and others repeat the problem on another register, insofar as they finesse the phenomenon of duration and exemplify in their stillness all that cinema sought to overcome in its illusion of motion. Would that the web overcame the hurdles of copyright so that you could read this with "live" streams.) This summary means, then, to spur you toward more watching, more listening, more reading, more thinking about what you see and hear. That said, there is no other chapter-length summary like it. It moves quickly and might function nicely as a reference to which you may wish to return.

FILM ANALYSIS, THE BASICS: *MISE-EN-SCÈNE*

We start with **mise-en-scène**. From the French – not a bad language to sharpen if you're drawn to cinema studies – in its initial use it meant the theatrical process of staging. In film study it retains the theatrical overtones, meaning to "put into the scene" and designating all that encompassed by the **frame** (the bounded axes of the image, discussed in the section on "Cinematography;" see pp. 36–42). In the study of *auteurs*, you will recall, it was in *mise-en-scène* that the French intellectuals found the evidence for authorial signatures and individual genius, but it is also in *mise-en-scène* that we often find a palpable manifestation of what we might call in the vernacular the "world of the film," its feel, its attitude toward detail, its sense of its own reality against which we can measure its representations. It thus provides a useful starting point for describing what you're seeing. If viewers of Edward D. Wood, Jr.'s *Plan 9 From Outer Space* (1959) observe gleefully that the "flying saucer" is in reality a metal pie plate suspended by a visible string, Wood's earnest world of zombies and space travel, like many of the

B-films spoofed on television's *Mystery Science Theater 3000*, nonetheless retains its own wacky logic and appeal. Remember, in other words, that "reality" partakes of the *functions* of *mise-en-scène* more than the measurement of its elements against a presumed "real world," at the same time as films summon our experience of living in that real world by way of our reactions and responses. In order to parse out how *mise-en-scène* establishes a film's world through its visual style, it helps to divide its categories. There are six components to *mise-en-scène* if you believe strongly, as I do, that "hair" deserves its very own, to wit: setting (set and props), lighting, costume, hair, make-up, and figure behavior.

SETTING

Setting needn't be constructed, although it often is. It refers to the streets of Dakar in Senegal, the city from which the characters Mory and Anta in Djibril Diop Mambety's film odyssey *Touki Bouki* (1973) begin a journey toward an imaginary France (referenced in the film through Josephine Baker's song "Paris, Paris, Paris," looped on the soundtrack), just as much as it refers to the Los Angeles suburbs in which hundreds of B-westerns allege to have found "New Mexico" or "Arizona." It refers to Victorian London as it is conjured through the smoky, gritty street scenes of the BBC production of Sarah Waters' quasi-lesbian novel *Tipping the Velvet* (2004), as much as it refers to the pop-shorthand version of "London" on offer in *Austin Powers: The Spy Who Shagged Me* (Jay Roach, 1999), with its impromptu pre-shagging Elvis Costello number, red telephone booths, and groovy double-deckers. Shooting on **location** – that is, using settings found in the world rather than constructed in the studio – does not mean that the world of the film thus created is not constructed or is simply "realistic." Just think, as the joke goes, of how many apartment windows in films that take place in Paris just happen to feature a stunning view of the Eiffel Tower. Location shooting relies on deliberate choices to enlist the help of already-constructed locales in the production of the film's setting. Wynn Thomas, the production designer for Spike Lee's *Do the Right Thing* (1989), masterminded the painstaking "recreation" of an actual block in the Bedford-Stuyvesant neighborhood of Brooklyn to use as the

Figure 2.1: Do the Right Thing.
Source: Universal/The Kobal Collection.

film's setting (see Figure 2.1). Another option, frequently used for narrative films with significant budgets, is the studio shoot on a **sound stage** (a built locale in which every variable of light and sound can be calculated to simulate whatever environment a filmmaker wishes to create). Sets are not confined to measurable interiors, such as dwellings or workplaces, but can extend literally into the new worlds of galaxies and universes beyond our own.

If settings often blend found and constructed elements, **props** (short for "properties") help to amplify a mood, give further definition to a setting, or call attention to detail within the larger scene. In Hitchcock's *Psycho* (1960), stuffed game birds peering down upon Norman Bates and Marion Crane in the Bates Motel define the word "creepy," but they also give away the secret of the film (see Figure 2.2). (I won't reveal it here if you haven't seen the film.) Props can serve an overt narrative function. In an early American narrative film such as D.W. Griffith's *The Lonedale Operator* (1911), the actress Blanche Sweet fends off two robbers who are after a mining company's payroll money, delivered to the train station at which she serves as telegraph operator. The film's punch line comes when the robbers learn that her "weapon" had all along

Figure 2.2: *Psycho*.
Source: Paramount/The Kobal Collection.

been a wrench, masquerading in the dark as a gun. (You may practice your own psychoanalytic interpretation of what this "weapon"
might represent at home.) In early prints of the film, Griffith **tinted**
(colored) the wrench to stand out against the dusky night, so that

spectators would experience Sweet's captivity as suspense, in fear that her ruse might be exposed. Props can also serve less overt narrative functions, condensing meaning without declaring it baldly. To take another mining example, in the final shot of Douglas Sirk's wonderfully perverse melodrama *Written on the Wind* (1956) Marylee Hadley (Dorothy Malone) strokes a replica of an oil derrick as she assumes the position of family matriarch. In this story of a Texas oil family's debauchery and fall (a precursor to the television serials *Dallas* and *Dynasty*, to be sure) the erect phallus can only be an artificial one!

LIGHTING

Lighting, just as effectively as props, establishes mood and directs attention to detail. Obvious examples of extreme variations in lighting include the German expressionist film *The Cabinet of Dr. Caligari* (1920), wherein fear and menace reveal themselves through angular sets and *chiaroscuro* (bold contrasts between light and dark) interiors and street scenes, or in the post-war American film movement known as *film noir*, ("dark film"), literally as descriptive of its settings in urban crime and mystery, and figuratively as descriptive of its investigations of shady lives and dark themes inaugurating the post-war landscape. These two examples disclose the extent to which lighting is often naturalized, thought of as emanating naturally from a film's setting. Perhaps because spectators frequently know little about how lighting works, or perhaps because filmmakers now manipulate it so effectively that we are drawn in by the illusion, we frequently overlook its power in the experience of cinema.

In fact, however, even the effect of naturalistic lighting in cinema takes an enormous amount of work, relying upon the repertoire of effects possible through the system of **three-point lighting**, developed during the studio era in Hollywood and largely dominant still today. As the name suggests, the system describes three sources of lighting, and is reliant upon a **key light**, a **fill light**, and a **backlight** in order to balance the lighting for effect in any given shot setup. Also commonsensically, the key light provides the primary or key light source. It tends to illuminate most strongly the shot's subject, and it also tends to cast the strongest shadows. A fill light, which might be positioned near the camera roughly 120° or thereabouts from the key light, literally "fills in" the shadows thrown by the key light. Compensating for the key light's strength and tendency to throw harsh shadows, the fill light softens the illumination upon the subject and its surrounding area. The backlight, finally, comes from behind the subject (in our example roughly another 120° from the fill light) and separates the subject from the background, counterbalancing the brightness of the key light. By varying the intensities and direction of light through the three-point system, filmmakers achieve an astounding variety of effect, from the even **high-key** lighting of the classical Hollywood cinema (wherein little contrast between bright and dark obtains, soft and revealing of detail) to the **low-key** (high contrast, harsh, and hard) lighting frequently used in horror and mystery (including my previous examples drawn from *noir*). In the former case, the high-key style contributes to a worldview that values transparency, clarity, intelligibility; the most extreme example of high-key lighting is the television situation comedy. In the latter case, lighting helps to gesture toward the underworld, the shadowy world, uncertainty, fear, or evil.

Lighting helps viewers to understand setting as well as the characters and actors within that setting. Throwing a light under a character's face, underlighting, creates a spooky or sinister effect, for example, whereas positioning a light behind the subject by **backlighting** may create a halo around the hair, suggesting the character's saintliness. Special kinds of lighting magnify the best that stars have to offer: a **kicker** (backlighting on the subject's temple) reveals chiseled cheekbones, while an **eye light** (lighting from the front, from a light placed on the camera) creates a glamorous twinkle. But films use other cues to build our perceptions of characters, both principal and marginal. **Costume**, in tandem with setting and props, delineates the world of a film and its characters, too.

COSTUME AND HAIR

Genre, a term designating films of a common type, provides an easy inroad to costuming: we can think easily of a cowboy's look as he rides into town in a western, or of a spaceship officer's garb as she sits before a flashing control board in a science fiction film. Because genre is an effect of repetition, we learn its codes so that we can quickly orient ourselves to the new iteration of a given story. This form of "typing" is not limited to genre films, of course. Sergei Eisenstein's *The Battleship Potemkin* (1925) exploits "**typage**" in order to differentiate the heroic sailors from the rigid and oppressive officers on the battleship. The brawny sailors (actual sailors cast for type) wear white and gleam as brightly as the ship's brass they polish proudly, while the officers' dark uniforms amplify their sinister tendencies and hawk-like preying upon the enlisted men. And Eisenstein's awareness of the importance of **hair** styling reveals itself through the outrageous wig worn by the character of the ship's priest, his outdated fanaticism emblematized in his wild locks. Details of costuming contribute to the believability of a film's world, in other words, but good costume design is not simply about historical fidelity or accuracy. "Unless of course the film requires it, I'm not interested in an exact replica of the period," remarks Sandy Powell, one of the most accomplished designers in film's history. "I look at the period, how it should be, how it could be, and then I do my own version" (Bellafante 1999: 82).

MAKE-UP

Make-up often goes unnoticed in many realist films. Indeed, it became recognized as an art with its own category for the Academy Awards as late as 1965. Epic historical films, such as Mel Gibson's *Braveheart* (1995), or large-scale fantasy or science fiction productions, such as the *Star Wars* and *Lord of the Rings* cycles, clearly draw attention to the role of make-up in creating imaginative dimensions of the film world. But make-up is one of those elements of the larger effect of **glamor**, which by definition remains concealed as a process and as labor. Star images depend upon the idea that stars "naturally" look better than mere mortals, and that their beauty shines forth with or without the efforts of a crew in the make-up truck. In Billy Wilder's brilliant satire of Hollywood life *Sunset Boulevard.* (1950), aging actress Norma Desmond (Gloria Swanson, herself a silent era legend) undergoes a barrage of facial treatments, muscle exercises, and the like in the belief that she is on the threshold of a comeback. Wilder reveals how her star image is constructed through hard work that is then rendered invisible through the mechanics of film stardom. It is of course true that actors are selected for their looks, whether glamorous or not, and that make-up aids in creating surfaces particularly congenial to be photographed. As Robert Towne observes, actors communicate powerfully through their screen presences:

> For gifted movie actors affect us most, I believe, not by talking, fighting, fucking, killing, cursing or cross-dressing. They do it by being photographed. . . . Great movie actors have features that are ruthlessly efficient. . . . The point is that a fine actor on screen conveys a staggering amount of information before he ever opens his mouth.
>
> (Dunne 1997: 160)

If their features are "ruthlessly efficient," that efficiency is augmented by the careful application of make-up for the process of photography.

FIGURE BEHAVIOR

Actors also do, of course, talk, fight, fuck, kill, curse and cross-dress: these various activities the sometimes deadening language of film analysis flattens into the category of **figure behavior**. Since *mise-en-scène* encompasses only those elements "put in" to the scene, figure behavior means to describe the movement, expressions, or actions of the actors or other figures (animals, monsters, animated things, droids) within a given shot. Acting *per se* thus receives little attention in formal analysis, which is instead concerned with the placement of figures within the frame, with narrative motivation for various forms of expression, with the production of affect through the face as an apparent window onto interior feeling or emotion, and with action that contributes to a film's narrative, its cause and effect logic. Danish director Carl-Theodor Dreyer's classic film *The Passion of Joan of Arc* (1928) records nuances of suffering and crisis as the martyred Joan is tried and subsequently hanged at Rouen Cathedral. Maria (Renée) Falconetti's performance, considered by many to be one of film's greatest, thus receives formal treatment less in terms of acting *style* than in terms of Dreyer's manipulation of point of view and use of the close-up of Falconetti's naked face (i.e. without make-up, which he forbade in the service of realism). As David Bordwell has shown in a remarkably careful reading of the film, Dreyer deploys the close-up precisely *not* in order to solicit identification with the martyred Joan, but instead to create a truly divine point of view or perspective of judgment that is distinct from *both* herself and her persecutors (Bordwell 1981).

CINEMATOGRAPHY

To notice any single element of *mise-en-scène* is also to notice an element of cinematography, since everything "put in" to a given shot is recorded by a camera. That camera, in turn, is placed to include some elements and to exclude others (to leave them offscreen in **offscreen space** or **implied space**). That decision involves the act of **framing** the **profilmic** event, or that which lies before the camera; even films that exist independently of a profilmic event (such as those experimental films discussed in Chapter 1) rely upon inclusion and exclusion for every frame. The camera records the shot at a given **camera distance** from the setting and its action. The camera chronicles the action from a fixed or changing **camera angle**. Even a stationary camera establishes and may change focus, in order to emphasize a particular plane or planes within the camera's **depth of field**, the three-dimensional space the camera's lens is capable of recording in focus in two dimensions, according to the shot's role and logic. And the camera's angle and distance may remain constant or change with the **camera's movement** during the shot. Anything to do with the camera, that is, belongs to the realm of cinematography.

Framing can be understood practically as well as philosophically; I find it one of the most important elements of cinema and one that opens onto other aspects of cinematography, following upon the insights of Gilles Deleuze, who notes that "the frame teaches us that the image is not just given to be seen. It is legible as well as visible" (Deleuze 1986: 12). Ronald Bogue, a particularly fine reader of Deleuze's work on cinema, summarizes five elements of framing we can isolate in order to explore its function:

1   In terms of content, it provides information. "The more information that fills the framed image," suggests Bogue, "the more it may be said to be 'saturated'; the less information, the more 'rarefied' the image becomes, until it reaches the limit of the empty black or white screen" (Bogue 2003: 42). If the film I mentioned in Chapter 1, *The Flicker*, represents the rarefied pole, Wes Anderson's stylized 2001 film *The Royal Tennenbaums* works well as an example of the saturated other extreme, crammed as every shot is with detail and visual information.

2   The frame itself, as limiting border, functions either geometrically or dynamically. In the first case, "the frame establishes a fixed compositional grid of horizontal, vertical, and diagonal coordinates" (Bogue 2003: 43) within which elements are organized. In the second, the frame functions dynamically with that which is framed. Hitchcock's framing of the fields of the American Midwest in *North by Northwest* relies on geometric framing; indeed, Hitchcock's own **storyboards**, the drawings that provide a graphic vision of each setup or shot, lay bare his interest in the frame's geometric function. **Canted framing**, in which the horizontal axis appears tilted, can also signal that something is "out of whack," such as Spike Lee's use of the canted frame (also called **Dutch angles**) in *Do the Right Thing* in order to indicate brewing tensions. By contrast, the use of iris shots in a film such as Germaine Dulac's *The Smiling Madame Beudet* (1922) reveals the subjective life of the trapped bourgeois woman of the title. As Alan Williams observes of this "grimly comic" tale, Dulac's use of props and subjective camera divulge the extent to which "the heroine has internalized her oppressive situation so completely that the ways in which she can rebel against it . . . only serve as humorous illustrations of her terrible psychic imprisonment" (Williams 1992: 147–8).

3   The frame both separates and unites the included elements: parts are related geometrically, parts related dynamically. The horizon consistently on display in the genre of the Hollywood western provides an example of the former,

while images of fog or shadows provide movement which can unite what remains within the frame dynamically.

4   Every frame implies an "angle of framing" or implicit point of view. This point of view may have narrative motivation (which I discuss at length soon; see pp. 119– 20), or it may provide a puzzle for the spectator to solve or ponder. From whose point of view or from what position am I seeing what is onscreen?

5   The frame both includes and excludes. Every frame determines an "out of field" beyond the framed image. Film critic Noel Burch distinguishes six spatial axes in the out of field: above or below the frame, to the right or left, in depth away from the camera or toward and beyond it. Deleuze proposes, in addition to the spatial out of field, an absolute out of field of *durée*, or duration.

Framing, of course, depends on other cinematographic choices. Every placement of the camera can be analyzed in terms of the distance between the camera and its object(s). Film analysis has evolved an anthropocentric taxonomy for describing distance, that is, using the human body as the reference point for each designation:

- the extreme long shot (ELS), in which one can barely distinguish the human figure;
- the long shot (LS), in which humans are distinguishable but remain dwarfed by the background;
- the medium long shot (MLS), or plan americain, in which the human is framed from the knees up;
- the medium shot (MS), in which we move in slightly to frame the human from the waist up;
- the medium close-up (MCU), in which we are slightly closer and see the human from the chest up;
- the close-up (CU), which isolates a portion of a human (the face, most prominently);
- and the extreme close-up (ECU), in which we see a mere portion of the face (an eye, the lips).

All of these designations can be brought to shots without humans in them, but the language of camera distance relies on a conception of the human in the frame in order to measure it. The height of the camera and its angle, as I have already noted, are also implicated in framing.

What we see of the object(s) in a given shot also depends upon the manipulation of light and of focus, in turn dependent, as with most types of photography, upon the selection of a camera's **lens** and the **film stock** for its sensitivity to light. Lenses come in different **focal lengths**, selected for their ability to alter perceptions of depth and scale: short focus (commonly called wide angle) lenses, which exaggerate depth (and which bend straight lines at the fringes of the frame, creating distortions such as the "fishbowl" effect); middle focal length lenses of up to 50mm, which avoid distortion and reproduce Renaissance perspective; and long focal length or telephoto lenses, which flatten depth and magnify events at a distance, allowing us to see details from very far away. Unlike these lenses with fixed focal lengths (called prime lenses), zoom lenses allow a cinematographer to change focal length over the course of a single shot; changing, or **racking**, focus in the course of a shot can simulate camera movement, in which we may appear to be closer to an object or person, moving from, say, a medium long shot to a close-up, but in fact the camera remains stationary while the cinematographer adjusts the focal length of the lens. Film stocks vary as to their responsiveness to amount and type of light source; the level of a film's **exposure** depends upon the calibration of light

BOX 2.1: *CITIZEN KANE* (WELLES, 1941)

Depth of field – an element of cinematography – combines with the construction of setting – an element of *mise-en-scène* – famously in Orson Welles' *Citizen Kane*. Cinematographer Gregg Toland captured the vast sets constructed to display Kane's opulent life in his mansion Xanadu in such a way as to keep many planes in sharp focus. The combination of short focal length lenses with very light-sensitive or fast film recording **deep space** came to be called, after *Kane*, **deep focus** and was used repeatedly throughout several decades.

Figure 2.3: The Woman in the Window.
Source: RKO/The Kobal Collection.

source, stock, and **aperture**, which both controls the amount of light to which the film is exposed and also determines **depth of field**, or those planes which remain in sharp focus in a given shot.

Cameras, of course, may move, on trains and in hot-air balloons, sometimes. They are mounted on jet airplanes and carried in pockets. Some are handheld, and some handheld cameras require the complicated scaffold of the Steadicam to give operators minute control and balance. Several forms of camera movement bear specific mention. When a camera rotates on its vertical axis – that is, when it remains stationary but for that rotation – we describe that movement as **panning**, frequently to scan a crowd or establish a vast space. When a camera rotates on its horizontal axis, again – when it remains stationary but for that rotation – the effect is **tilting**, frequently to establish a building's height or a view from a lower to a higher perspective. When the camera is freed from a stationary position, it becomes mobile and reframes, of course, as it moves. Such mobile framing, then, involves a camera which is said to be **traveling**: **dollying**, when it rests on a dolly or some other form of wheeled contraption (amateurs love wheelchairs, as they are cheap and accessible), **tracking**, when such a dolly travels on actual tracks laid on the set for that purpose, or, less frequently, **trucking**, as the camera rides on a truck or other vehicle on the ground. Such mobile framing can involve movement backward, forward, side to side, or around in circles, and can vary furthermore in terms of speed. When the camera leaves the ground, it is **craning**, frequently on an actual crane which lifts it from the ground to provide aerial perspective. Another famous Orson Welles innovation is the astonishing opening shot of *Touch of Evil* (1958), fully three minutes long, which sets up the locale of Tijuana and the action to follow in an incredible craning / tracking shot. Michael Snow's *Wavelength* (1967) introduces the psychedelic effects of what appears to be (but is not only) a zoom lens adjustment which takes *forty-five minutes* to travel across a room to a photograph pinned on the wall. **Shot duration**, then, becomes an important companion to mobile framing, determined only by the amount of film one can load into a camera's **magazine** for a single shot; duration has consequences for the spectator's relationship to the image such as I discussed in relation to the long take in Chapter 1.

One final aspect of the single shot that bears further mention before I move to the combination of shots through editing is the **process shot** or composite shot. These are created through the use of special effects in order to layer multiple images or strips of film into a single shot. The simple form of such layering can happen in the camera, by exposing a single strip of film twice or even multiple times, creating the effect of **superimposition**. Laboratories can create effects such as superimposition, used often to create "ghosts" or translucent effects, or more elaborate shots, such as the use of **rear projection** or front projection. Developed in the 1920s in order to cut the costs of filming on location, rear projection involved the use of a translucent screen, onto which location footage was projected and in front of which the actors played out the scene meant to take place in that location. Scenes of cars driving in 1930s cinema provide the paradigmatic example, the cause of mirth for spectators now who are alert to the unconvincing depth cues and mismatches in quality of image, lighting, and shadow that often characterize such composite shots. (We think of them now, in other words, as cheesy.) The answer to the degraded image projected from the rear appeared to lie in eliminating the screen as a mediator from the process. Front projection replaced the screen with a concave mirror, and a projector placed in the same position the camera occupied, throwing the *image* thus created onto a highly reflective screen (much improved with the invention in the 1950s of Scotchlite, a reflective material invented and manufactured by 3M). A beam-splitter was placed equidistant, and at 45°, between the camera and projector, which were situated at 90° to each other. **Matte shots** also combine multiple images into a single shot: static mattes, such as matte painting, replace a portion of the frame with an imaginary world superimposed upon it, while traveling mattes, frequently created through bluescreen processes, allow the actors to interact with the imported setting. Within a single shot, worlds combine.

EDITING

Thus far I have concentrated my discussion on the single shot, itself composed through choices in the areas of *mise-en-scène* and cine-matography. Very few films, not even *Wavelength*, contain only a single shot, however; most join many, many shots together. Aleksandr

BOX 2.2: COMPOSITING: BLUESCREEN

A special form of compositing involves the bluescreen tech-nique, in which foreground action is shot against an evenly lit blue background, then replaced by a separately shot background plate through optical compositing. Used most routinely by tele-vision weathermen and women (and parodied hilariously in *Anchorman: The Legend of Ron Burgundy* [Adam McKay, 2004]), bluescreen works well for human subjects because human skin has very little blue (or green) color in it, and computer-generated weather maps easily substitute as the back-ground plate. Inventor Petro Vlahos founded his company Ultimatte to build upon his original 1964 version of bluescreen processes and is now producing sophisticated compositing hard-ware and software for the film industry.

Sokurov's film *Russian Ark* (2002) indeed bears mention as the first feature film shot in a single, unbroken take, while at the other end of the continuum most Hollywood films employ shots fewer than ten seconds in duration. Scholar David Bordwell clocks the shot duration of most Hong Kong action films – typically featuring "spitting, vomiting, nose-picking and vistas of toilets and people's mouths" – at seven seconds (Bordwell 2000: 6). Editing is the general term designating the techniques and logic of joining shots together into larger strings or sequences; there are five different types of edits. The most common is the **cut**, in which the first shot cleanly ends where the second begins; the shots are spliced together using tape or cement. A **dissolve** joins two shots together by blending them, so that the end of the first shot and the beginning of the second shot are superimposed upon the screen for a period of time specified by the filmmaker to the laboratory. A fade may work in either of two directions: a **fade-in** lightens a shot from a black or otherwise colored screen, while a **fade-out** darkens to black. Fades often open and close films: fade to black, the end. The fourth type of edit, a **wipe**, involves a boundary line replacing the first shot with the second: it may be vertical or horizontal or some other sort of whimsical graphic. And you have already encountered the last type of edit, the iris, an opening or closing of the screen to a circle: that's all, folks.

It's not a bad idea to practice noticing editing, both watching for the presence of edits and learning which ones generally do what. Artificial though it is, I ask my students to say the word "shot" whenever they notice an edit while watching clips for a few days; others suggest clapping or tapping a pencil or your shoe. Whatever your preferred method, once you're able to distinguish edits and their functions, you'll discover that you can gain a feel for the pace of editing, thereby accessing the rhythmic possibilities of combination, and for the *function* of graphic, spatial, and temporal relationships between shots. These four areas (rhythmic, graphic, spatial, temporal) provide the framework for most discussions of how filmmakers shape sequences, and it's worth noticing how they work differently across different types of movies. Most films, for instance, conjoin shots of differing lengths together, but some films, and some sequences within films, create *patterns* of combination, producing recognizable rhythms with varying effects. Foreshortening shots can build momentum or suspense, for instance, while lengthening them can allow for release, meditation, or contemplation. Abstract films rely almost entirely on rhythmic editing and graphic editing to build their temporal and spatial worlds, while principles of graphic combination drive only some decisions in narrative films (although any juxtaposition of one image to another creates a graphic relationship between them). One dominant graphic basis for combination in narrative films is the **graphic match**, where graphic similarities in two shots provide the edit's justification. In narrative films, the temporal and spatial logics of combination tend to predominate, since narrative films build imaginary worlds that are more or less coherent in space and time.

Mise-en-scène and cinematography contribute to the sense of a film's world, but it is spatial editing that literally constructs film space for us, since films join shots together that may have been recorded in wildly different places to construct a sense of connection present only in the film. The continuity, in other words, is produced by and through film itself, an illusion, similar to the illusion of movement produced through the persistence of vision, first discovered before 1920 by the Soviet filmmaker Lev Kuleshov. He undertook a series of experiments in a short film in which shots of the face of Ivan Mozzhukhin (who was a Tsarist matinee idol) are juxtaposed with various other shots (a plate of soup, a girl, a child's coffin). The film's initial audience testified to Kuleshov that the expression on Mozzhukhin's face was different each time he appeared, depending on whether he was responding to the plate of soup (he appeared hungry), the girl (he appeared happy or desirous), or the child's coffin (he appeared sad or grieving), when in fact each instance of his appearance was identical (and the actor was meant to be blank, without expression). The "**Kuleshov effect**" has come for film scholars to describe the fact that, in the absence of an establishing shot, the audience will infer a spatial whole from a portion of space. The broader point, however, is that audiences create connections and combinations from fragments, retrospectively generating cause and effect logics or explanations where none was on offer, or creating continuous space from discrete images. Even in the presence of an establishing shot, such as that of an office building in Los Angeles in *Speed*, which precedes a sequence in which office workers go about their business, there is no reason to believe that the offices are located in that building in the actual world. The elevator, the workers, the exterior police cars, the interior SWAT team all may have been filmed in different locations or on different sets but edited together to generate "the office building" in the film's first suspenseful episode.

That sequence in *Speed* is an example of a pattern common in commercial narrative film: establishment, breakdown, re-establishment. In this pattern, the film offers a locale, the space in which action is to occur, and subsequently breaks down the space into its component parts, and then re-establishes the locale before moving to a different space. Another pattern, used to suggest simultaneous action in different spaces, is **cross-cutting**, or **parallel editing**, that moves from the action in one space to the action in another and back and forth. Commonly used to generate suspense, "cross-cutting" is the visual equivalent of "meanwhile." These commonplaces of spatial editing, as you can see, also therefore embed temporal relationships, which are augmented by editing that deliberately orients us to a film world's time. For narrative films present us with stories that take place over centuries, over decades, over years, over weeks, over days. Few films, that is, unwind in **real time**, in which screen time corresponds precisely to plot and **story time**. Chantal Akerman's 1976 film *Jeanne Dielman, 23 Quai du Commerce, 1080 Bruxelles* does so to make an ideological point, as it records many real-time activities of a Brussels widow going about her chores, producing for the spectator a painful and mind-numbing experience, ultimately then awakening them to this woman's oppression. Screen time, usually ninety to 120 minutes for a feature film, more often drastically condenses **story** time (where "story" is the whole world of the film, involving events both given and implied), so that what we actually see and hear (called the film's **plot**) cuts out huge swaths of a film's story. Those swaths constitute temporal ellipses, and temporal editing is both what controls them and what renders plot time intelligible for viewers. Temporal editing, then, is not simply to do with the ordering of events in the plot, though filmmakers do, of course, make decisions about the sequencing of events, the use of **flashbacks** (in which events that took place in the plot past are interwoven with those of the plot present) and **flashforwards** (the opposite case). Like framing, temporal editing invokes exciting questions about inclusion and exclusion, about what kind of cut in time the film seeks to make. Austrian *avant-garde* filmmaker Peter Kubelka remarks of his two-minute

1957 *Adebar* (a structural study of dancers at a Vienna disco set to Pygmy music) that it is a film not to be studied for its meaning but rather memorized; his interest lies in an interval without beginning or end but which is nonetheless seized and experienced as a temporal unfolding.

Most narrative films, by contrast, rely on very explicit beginnings, middles, and ends, and, as I have been suggesting, obey certain conventions in order to keep spectators oriented in time and space so that the narrative may unfold without distraction. The last area that therefore requires discussion with regard to editing, particularly the spatial and temporal editing I have been discussing, is the system of **continuity editing**, the name for the ensemble of those conventions solidified over time and so naturalized that one frequently only observes it as a system when it is violated. This is the system that solidifies in the classical Hollywood cinema, the name for a style of films that obey the strictures of continuity editing and that, furthermore, were produced under the Hollywood studios' profit-driven mode of film production by "serial manufacture" (involving the contributions of many differently skilled makers). Most viewers know its habits or its rules, then, even if they don't have names for them: the **axis of action** and **180° rule**, the **30° rule**, principles of shot combination based on spatial orientation such as the pattern of **shot–reverse shot** or the **match on action** or the **eyeline match**, and control of temporal ellipses through conventions associated with different types of edits and patterns of juxtaposition.

To preserve spatial continuity, editors rely upon patterns such as the establishment, breakdown, re-establishment pattern, but they also build spatial relationships through the maintenance of perspective on the action as it unfolds. Imagine filming a martial arts fight, in which the master and his challenger duel on the side of a lake (as in Ang Lee's *Crouching Tiger, Hidden Dragon* [2000]). In order to preserve the spectator's understanding of **screen direction** (what's left, what's right, who's who in the space, and who's heading in what direction), encircle the space with a line, then draw a line dividing the circle into two hemispheres. Now film all of the action on one side of your line, on one side of the axis of action: each time the master kicks, she will move from screen left, unless we *see* her switch places with the challenger. Each time the challenger jumps, he will jump from screen right, with the same exception. By following the 180° rule, always filming from one side of the axis of action, you will keep the spectator oriented, thereby warding off puzzlement that might interrupt his or her immersion in the story. The 30° rule suggests that changes in camera angle ought to be greater than 30°; otherwise, a cut between angles too similar to one another will result in a **jump cut**, an effect exploited by the French New Wave in which a character appears to jump slightly in the frame. Similarly also to the pattern of breaking down space, conversations between characters follow patterns, in which two characters appear in a shot together before an editor will alternate shots of individual characters, returning now and again to the two-shot. This **shot–reverse shot** pattern reminds the spectator that the characters, even if shown alone, occupy the same space (or have a virtual connection, so that telephone conversations work through cross-cutting). And if a character looks toward space that is offscreen, an **eyeline match** dictates that the next shot will show us what the character there sees, uniting expanding screen space and locating characters within it simultaneously. Finally, also to expand screen space, a **match on action** follows a character's action into a new space: we see a character from a home's exterior, responding to a doorbell and opening the door. In a match on action, the following shot finds us inside the home, watching the guest enter the hallway. The goal, again: to orient, to allay anxiety over discontinuity that might detract from the story. It's the same house, the film says; don't worry, we're just inside now.

Continuity editing also works to dispel worries about temporal ellipses. Explicit cues signal shifts in time. Flashbacks may require editing cues such as dissolves or graphic matches (a house now and then), if not titles on screen ("Eight years earlier"). The passage of time forward also follows conventions in the use of edits: cuts tend to suggest continuous, linear action unfolding in time, whereas dissolves and, more dramatically, fades move us from an evening to a morning, or from one week to another. Props help, of course: the old fan-blowing-on-a-calendar trick helped to communicate the passage of significant amounts of time, just as the bold LED display on a ticking bomb helps us understand just how much time our hero has to defuse it. Another way to condense time involves editing together shots of sufficient similarity to create a sense of repetition over time; in a **montage sequence** (as distinct from Sergei Eisenstein's theory of montage) a series of news headlines, or a

BOX 2.3: FAMOUS CONTINUITY ERRORS

Fans track continuity errors more effectively than do directors, apparently. Websites devoted to "movie mistakes" keep count (145 for *Spiderman* alone on www.moviemistakes.com!), and clearly the ability to spot errors in continuity develops early on as one learns the grammar of narrative cinema. There is, no doubt, a certain pleasure in mastery involved in noticing a window magically intact after being shattered in the previous shot, a knowingness that is perhaps augmented by the additional awareness of the vast sums of money spent in the making of films meant to wow us with their flawlessness and their capacity for manipulation of the image. A few spotted and reported by fans in *Spiderman* are:

> Continuity: The intact windows mentioned above – in the scene where Mary Jane is being mugged by four men, Spiderman throws two of the men into two windows behind Mary Jane. Then the camera goes back to Spiderman beating up the other two guys. When the camera goes back to Mary Jane the two windows are intact.
>
> Continuity: When Peter shoots his web at his bedroom lamp and pulls it across the room, it smashes against the wall and breaks. But when Aunt May is talking to Peter from the door seconds later, the lamp is back on the dresser in one piece.
>
> Continuity: In the scene where Norman is getting ready to test himself he lays down on the bed, fastens himself in and the doctor goes to the computer. However, when it shows him being brought into the chamber he has several electrodes connected to his chest and head.
>
> Visible crew/equipment: When Peter stands up after being bitten by the spider, there's the reflection of the cameraman with headphones on the television set behind him.
>
> Continuity: In the final cemetery sequence, Peter and Mary Jane square off for a little heart to heart, with her touching his face tenderly with her black leather

gloves. The camera cuts between front views of both: in hers, her fingers are touching his ear lobe, in his, they are an inch below his ear lobe. In one quick cut of hers, the hand has disappeared completely, then in midsentence, as they cut back to Peter, it's there again. Factual error: When Harry is talking to Mary Jane on the phone, she hangs up on him and his cell phone produces a dial tone. Cell phones do not have a dial tone.

series of performances, or a series of breakfast table conversations (all of which Welles uses in *Kane*), efficiently compress story time, using, however, little screen time. Keeping spectators oriented in time, these devices insure the smooth unfolding of the story in whatever order seems best suited for its purposes.

SOUND

The fan's final example of an error in continuity in *Spiderman* alerts us to the construction and manipulation not only of visual worlds but aural ones, in all forms of film, and these worlds interact dynamically. Sound, however, engages a distinct sensory realm worth attending to with some specificity, even (or perhaps especially) when silence seems to prevail. Sound, as many critics have taught us, functions in a variety of different ways. Not mere accompaniment to the image, sound actively shapes how we perceive and interpret the image. It directs our attention within the image, and it cues us to form expectations. Just as elements of the image function as motifs, so too do elements or types of sound. Just as images harden quickly into clichés, so too do elements or types of sound: thunder cracks to announce a storm, car tires squeal to signal a criminal getaway, explosions in space make "kaboom" noises, and so on.

Although these examples suggest a wide range of sound elements, in the language of formal analysis there are only three types of film sound: speech, music, noise (effects). Speech is not restricted to dialogue, although dialogue is one of narrative film's most compelling devices, stitching the actor to the character and rendering that character knowable through the texture of the voice to the audience. Speech in film can serve other masters than naturalism, too: as the great Soviet director V.I. Pudovkin understood, sound may offer a counterpoint rather than an accompaniment to an image, a subjective route to understand an objective visual presentation. Likewise, dialogue links human speech to the broader acoustic world in which we live, to the "vast conversational powers of life," as film theorist Bela Balazs puts it. Speech brings us closer to the subtlety of emotion: a quiver in a child's voice, or an acoustic "close-up" on a belly laugh bring us into intimate association with the lifeworlds the screen portrays.

Since speech frequently emanates from onscreen characters, it is most frequently **diegetic** sound; that is, sound whose source belongs to the imaginative world of the film, sound that is understood to issue from that world rather than ours. Examples of **non-diegetic** sound include **voice-over** commentary (that is, commentary that issues from another world than that depicted on the screen), music that accompanies the image from without rather than from a source within the world of the film (music, that is, which we presume the characters do *not* hear), or noises on the soundtrack likewise there for the ears of the audience alone. The distinction between diegetic and non-diegetic sound helps us to understand how sounds in narrative film are motivated, how the sound design is constructed. Music can be understood to be non-diegetic, laid over the image for our ears alone as in Cameron Crowe's music-filled *Elizabethtown* (2005), until a shot of a car radio alerts us to the fact that what seemed non-diegetic was in fact diegetic sound (Tom Petty, Elton John, Ryan Adams, Patty Griffin) important to our understanding of the film's characters and their emotional journeys. Music, then, may serve in similar fashion to speech to cue us to emotion, and it can devolve just as easily into cliché; in melodrama, for example, the short, sharp bursts of orchestral music that cue the villain's entry are called "stings." But music may also serve to complicate a film's narrative, such as the paranoid search for the origins of sound in Francis Ford Coppola's film about surveillance, *The Conversation* (1974), or the illegal possession of the woman's voice in Jean-Jacques Beineix's *Diva* (1981). And finally, a musical **score** might stand on its own, as director Sidney Lumet, who generally believed that a score should serve a picture,

BOX 2.4: MAKING SOUND WORK

Another moment from Lumet's chronicle of movie-making illustrates how carefully editors construct sound (and how, sometimes, sound and image *don't* work together):

> The sound editor on *Murder on the Orient Express* hired the "world's greatest authority" on train sounds. He brought me the *authentic* sounds of not only the Orient Express but the Flying Scotsman, the Twentieth Century Limited, every train that had ever achieved any reputation. He worked for six *weeks* on train sounds only. His greatest moment occurred when, at the beginning of the picture, the train left the station at Istanbul. We had the steam, the bell, the wheels, and he even included an almost inaudible click when the train's headlights went on. He swore that all the effects were authentic. When we got to the mix (the point at which we put *all* the sound tracks together), he was bursting with anticipation. For the first time, I heard what an incredible job he'd done. But I had also heard Richard Rodney Bennett's magnificent music score for the same scene. I knew one would have to go. They couldn't work together. I turned to Simon. He knew. I said, "Simon, it's a great job. But, finally, we've heard a train leave the station. We've never heard a train leave the station in three-quarter time."
>
> (Lumet 1995: 184–5)

observes of the great Prokofiev score for Eisenstein's film *Alexander Nevsky*:

> The only movie score I've heard that can stand on its own as a piece of music is Prokofiev's "Battle on the Ice" from *Alexander Nevsky*. I'm told that Eisenstein and Prokofiev talked about it well before shooting began and that some of the composing was started before shooting. . . . Even when I hear the music on a record today, I start remembering the sequence visually. The two, music and picture, are indelibly linked: a great sequence, a great score.
>
> (Lumet 1995: 171)

Finally, "noise" encompasses a world of sound beyond those sounds we think of as "special" effects. As I show in Chapter 3, the world of noise is an intricately built scaffold supporting the broader feel of a film's world. Every footstep, every door slam, every pin drop is engineered in order to produce an acoustic landscape in a given film; not a single element of noise is simply natural or given. If the sound coming from the floor above in a hotel room is audible, it is meant to be audible in order to give our hero and heroine the chance for an accidental encounter; if we hear the voices of our stars rising above the din on a crowded street, it is so that we eliminate the buzz of real human noise to concentrate on their plight. Even ambient sound is recorded in order to be manipulated at the editing stage so as to answer to the sound designer's conception of the final product, whether that conception is edgy or predictable.

Film analysis has terms to characterize variations in acoustic properties common to speech, music, and noise: loudness (changes in volume, sometimes indicated by the perceived distance of the sound source), pitch (the perceived "highness" or "lowness" of a sound), timbre (the texture or feel of a sound; a "nasal" or "whiny" quality of a voice, for example). Further dimensions of film sound include rhythm (beat, pulse, pace, tempo, or pattern of accents), fidelity (the extent to which film sound is faithful, according to our conventional expectations, to its source), and space (not simply whether a sound is diegetic or non-diegetic but how sound shapes the space of what is filmed, how sound creates and defines space). Sound designers and editors manipulate all of these dimensions of film sound through principles of selection, combination, and alter-ation. Just as you might watch a sequence in order to describe elements of its *mise-en-scène* or the rhythm of its edits, so you might repeat a sequence several times over to begin to understand the principles undergirding its sound construction. And now that you have most of the tools you'll need to undertake formal analysis, put them to test all together: begin to use them to develop an *argument* about the film's formal construction. To do so, you'll want also to situate a film historically, a task I discuss in Chapter 3.

BOX 2.5: SUMMARY

The language of film analysis aids in our task of watching films closely to notice their construction. We may isolate six elements of what is "put in" to a given shot, or of *mise-en-scène*: setting, lighting, costume, hair, make-up, and figure behavior. Cinematography encompasses all that is to do with the camera: framing, angle, focus, movement, and compositing. The five types of edits (cut, dissolve, fade, wipe, and iris) serve different functions in different contexts, whether within the system of continuity editing associated with the narrative form of classical Hollywood cinema or other cinematic contexts. Finally, the three types of sound (speech, music, and noise) actively shape how we work with images. Experiment with readings of brief sequences to practice the terminology: once it comes quickly and easily, start to put it to use!

3

THE HISTORY OF FILM

The aim of this chapter is to present film history while simultane-ously understanding film *as* history. The practice of film history, in other words, is not understood as itself a transparent or linear march of progress as charted by critics but instead as a practice by filmmakers and scholars alike of *generating* history. This approach provides the best way I've been able to come up with for addressing the imbrication of film *with* history, with historical understanding as an engagement with the past. It is necessary perhaps to say this right up front, since it's an unorthodox emphasis in introductory approaches to film history, most of which simply survey crucial moments in the development of the cinema as a modern art form, industry, and social institution.

What I seek to emphasize alongside, not in place of, such an overview, first, is the way that we see image *as history* and recall history *as image*. Much of what we know of the past, in other words, we access through the vast archives of the cinema. In terms of the ontology of the cinema (outlined in Chapter 1's discussion of André Bazin), we watch with the knowledge that what appears had *been there*, had actually stood before the camera. In one way or another, every film from 1977, whether *Star Wars*, *Saturday Night Fever*, or

That Obscure Object of Desire, records "the 1970s," insofar as R2D2, John Travolta, and Fernando Rey stood before the camera to be fixed in time. Similarly, as David Forgacs remarks in his book on the film, Roberto Rossellini's *Rome, Open City* (1945) and subsequent films by that director evocatively function as a documentary record:

> It includes photographic evidence of Rome at the end of the Second World War. It shows what the city and its inhabitants looked like in 1945 and it shows something of what the war did to the city, notably in the various shots of bomb-damaged buildings. In Rossellini's next two films his camera crews would again photograph cities just after the war: the second episode of *Paisà* shows Naples, with the rubble of a bombed building and the cave of Mergelina where displaced families were housed; the fourth episode shows ruined buildings in Florence with the dome of San Lorenzo in the distance; *Germany Year Zero* photographs the devastated center of Berlin (the exteriors were filmed in the French Sector) where organ music drifts from a half-destroyed church, children play football in front of ruins and make their hideouts in the cavities of gutted buildings.
>
> (Forgacs 2000: 22)

But what, we now need to ask, do we make of how these films seize and respect the real? What do we know and what are we to make of these moments in their social, aesthetic, consequential dimensions?

We also recall history through images. Think of the 1950s. What do you see? A Technicolor suburb? Black-and-white footage of school integration? A rousing musical? Or think of Hiroshima or Nagasaki: a black-and-white mushroom cloud, grainy and brief? Think of industrial labor, and you perhaps witness molten steel pouring in a darkened factory, or their smokestacks bellowing, or workers streaming into factory gates. If you were not there, the camera was, and it enables your intimacy, proximity, witnessing of history's unfolding.

Second, film shapes history as much as it records or reflects it. Most directly, propaganda films – those films produced directly by the state – rally troops for war, advocate for sweeping national policy changes, stitch empires together, quell dissent. So, too, do commercial films, if less overtly, if less didactically, if less visibly intertwined with state power. Commercial films undergo censorship, often receive governmental subsidies, enter into labyrinths of legal regulation and intellectual property restrictions: all axes of state control. Experimental and *avant-garde* films, too, oftentimes give voice to what the commercial cinema suppresses; as scholar David James argues about American 1960s films, even the most abstract works, therefore, situate themselves in and of their times as "allegories" of cinema more broadly understood (James 1989). To recall film history, then, is to recall *our* history, as well as moments of particular brilliance and technological innovation. It is to recall how upbeat musicals, such as the vehicles for Fred Astaire and Ginger Rogers, provided relief and distraction to some from the woes of the depression in the 1930s. It is to recall how images of extreme violence, such as those in Quentin Tarantino's *Reservoir Dogs* (1992), rendered worried parents into activists, intervening into the distribution of rap music and music videos alongside commercial films. It is to recall how nations devastated by war rebuild their webs of popular connection through films such as Emir Kusturica's celebration of Serbia, *Life is a Miracle* (2004). And it is to recall how everyday gestures, acts, feelings, and responses feed from the cinematic machine and recycle through our own perceptions and senses.

To tell the story of the history of cinema, this chapter is organized into two sections, each of which generates different critical questions by investigating a different method of writing and filming history. The first, "Periodization," presents a schematic overview of several key moments in the history of cinema according to the paradigms that govern scholarly approaches to film history: invention, periodization according to decades, periodization by event, and industrial periodization via technological innovation. Each moment is meant both to stimulate deeper thinking about how viewers, makers, and critics systematize and organize historical understanding and to cast a critical glance at the generalizations that tend to emerge from such periodizing. The second section, "National cinemas," introduces the other significant paradigm that organizes film history, and it takes several key national cinemas as instances to illustrate the benefits and also the perils of the national model: British (Hammer) horror, the Nigerian video film, Italian "spaghetti" westerns, and the Indian (Bollywood) popular cinema. The second section is less an argument about the limits of national cinematic paradigms in an "age of globalization" than it is a demonstration of how knowledge of the politics of nation enriches one's understanding of films that *move,* that *circulate* internationally. It is nonetheless true that the global nature of the colonizing process (co-eval with the first half-century of cinema) and, as critics Ella Shohat and Robert Stam put it, "the global reach of the contemporary media virtually oblige the cultural critic to move beyond the restrictive framework of the nation-state" (Shohat and Stam 1994: 6). In emphasizing the benefits and drawbacks of a model of film history as waves of successive national movements, this section opens routes for understanding previous formations as transnational or international ones, and for recognizing new political, social, and cultural formations (i.e. European popular film and the European Union, Latin American cinemas and issues of cultural policy, and Asian popular cinemas, to name a few).

PERIODIZATION

In Chapter 1, you saw how cinema emerged from dazzling experiments in motion at the end of the nineteenth century, congealing into forms familiar to us very quickly after its birth around 1895. Birth, origins, invention; perhaps because cinema remains a relatively young medium, having just celebrated its centennial, scholars and makers return repetitively, if not obsessively, to the origins of cinema in search of its *essence.* Is it, at its core, motion? Is it memory? Mortality? Illusion? Vision? Perception? Storytelling? Love? Fantasy? In a marvelous experiment of the celebration and exploration of these origins, forty filmmakers worked with the original camera of the Lumière brothers (the box, if you recall, they dubbed the Cinématographe) for a 1996 film called *Lumière et compagnie / Lumière and Company,* well worth the effort made to screen it. Spike Lee, Neil Jordan, Liv Ullman, David Lynch, Gaston Kaboré, Sven Nykvist, Zhang Yimou; the leading lights of the modern cinema returned to the simple box the Lumière brothers invented to record and then to project films slightly shorter than a mere minute. What emerges in this homage to cinema's invention? A sense of cinema's possibility, a sense of wonder, a sense of awe: almost anything can unfold in a fifty-two-second interval. But also a sense of repetition with endless variation on the early films made by the Lumières: a kiss (but now between two young people with Down syndrome), a story (but now an elaborate dream spun from the singularly bizarre and midget-obsessed imagination of David Lynch), a myth (but now shifting from Western classicism to Burkina Faso), a crowd (but now peering into the camera reflexively and aware). If film historians seek to capture this stream of repetition and innovation, their task is to correlate these complex syncopations and counterpoints with the histories with which they intersect (that is, histories of nations, of individuals, of industries) and with flows that frequently evade the writing of history (those everyday or aleatory events elided by the stories of grand events and historical breaks).

Cinema's youth lends itself to periodization by decade, a useful, even, and symmetrical way of carving up a century-plus of film history, if a method we also ought to contest precisely for its reliance on these seemingly equivalent chunks of the past. How to approach a decade, then? The critical school called **historicism** (more specifically in literary studies called the new historicism) posits that a work of art can best be understood contextually, rather than as an autonomous product of an individual mind or hand. By locating an artwork in its time, place, and circumstance, historicists tend to explain its particular features as indebted to its milieu, its influences, and its local peculiarities. Unlike **Marxists**, who tend to see a cultural work's features as tied tightly to the **mode of production** (such as the studio system) under which it emerged, or to the economic system (such as late capitalism) in which it is located, historicists find multiple (and sometimes diffuse) determinations that help to mold an artwork's form and destiny. By way of example, the "Screen Decades" project characterizes each decade of American cinema with an overarching set of themes or preoccupations, some of which link to industrial history, others of which act as narrower frames for reading particular films. The following blurb encapsulates an idea of "the 1950s" in American cinema:

> From cold war hysteria and rampant anticommunist witch hunts to the lure of suburbia, television, and the new consumerism, the 1950s was a decade of sensational commercial possibility coupled with dark nuclear fears and conformist politics. Amid this amalgamation of social, political, and cultural conditions, Hollywood was under siege:

from the Justice Department, which pressed for big film companies to divest themselves of their theater holdings; from the middleclass, whose retreat to family entertainment inside the home drastically decreased the filmgoing audience; and from the House Un-American Activities Committee, which was attempting to purge the country of dissenting political views. In this difficult context, however, some of the most talented filmmakers of all time, including John Ford, Alfred Hitchcock, Vincente Minnelli, Nicholas Ray, and Billy Wilder, produced some of their most remarkable work.

(promotion material for Rutgers University Press's "Screen Decades" series)

While this view of the 1950s in America seems reasonable enough on first glance, even the landmarks upon which the volume relies to chart its monumental moments beg our attention. If the Justice Department enforced anti-monopoly legislation commanding studios to shed their theater chains, it did so by virtue of the 1948 Supreme Court *Paramount* decision, which came after more than twenty years of intensive anti-trust pressure. If the middle class retreated to the home, it was in large measure a white middle class who left the inner cities and now-decaying movie palaces to those African-Americans who settled in northern cities after the Great Migration of the 1920s and who had been banned from the suburbs by restrictive covenants (real-estate ownership and leasing agreements that preserved white residency). And if the House Un-American Activities Committee stepped up its pressure on Hollywood filmmakers, the McCarthy Senate hearings represented only the tail end of governmental pressure on left-wing organizations, since culture workers from the 1920s and 1930s faced red-baiting and sabotage, too, and McCarthy's hearings furthermore resulted in precisely zero convictions or criminal prosecutions for espionage. If "the 1950s" acts as an heuristic, a useful way to get started in thinking about patterns and contexts, it also immediately reveals strong connections both forward and backward that unravel its coherence. Film scholar Wheeler Winston Dixon's book *Lost in the Fifties* in fact explores through more esoteric films – such as *The Bigamist* (1953), directed by that rarity in Hollywood, a woman (named Ida Lupino) – a darker side of the decade than that glorified by Hollywood or many of its critics. Similarly, "the 1960s" as an international phenomenon bursts at its own seams, trying to capture films of anti-colonial struggles from the 1950s in Africa and Latin America; popular culture phenomena from the Beatles to surf movies to the seeds of "blaxploitation" (a portmanteau of the words "black" and "exploitation" used to characterize a genre of black-cast action films); counterculture; and feminism, the anti-war movement, the Black Power movement, the New Left, and so on. In terms of experimental film, the 1920s bleed into the 1930s. In terms of films about AIDS, the 1980s spill into the 1990s. And countless others ooze similarly beyond the confines of their ten-year barriers.

Marking periods by parameters other than decade yields other, oftentimes more fruitful, ways of understanding context. Studying the cinema of the Third Reich or of Italian fascism, for example, raises questions about the relationship between the state and civil society when the totalitarian or authoritarian government nationalizes or partially nationalizes a film industry in order to promote its vision. Certainly propaganda films emerged from both regimes; the images of stormtroopers, fascist salutes, and brownshirts are etched deeply in the historical record and in widespread recollections of the period. Even Hitler and Mussolini, however, nourished genres and stars many of us would be surprised to associate with fascism: Germany's melodramas and musicals starring Zarah Leander (even one, *La Habanera*, directed by the man who would become Douglas Sirk when he Americanized his German name, Dietlef Sierck) or the Italian comedies known as the *telefoni bianchi* (for, in order to show-case the comforts of the bourgeois household, there frequently appeared a white telephone). The co-existence of films easily under-stood as propaganda, producing and reproducing the people's allegiance to the ruling government, and films less easily understood as dogmatic or univocal helps us to complicate our understanding of how fascism itself works, how consent is manufactured, how resist-ance is coded, and how popular culture contributes to social and political analysis. In other words, studying an epoch's films sheds light on the larger phenomenon, while isolating an epoch for film history may reveal coeval film practices that generate greater understanding of film's *function* at any given moment.

To use a metaphor drawn from cinematography, if one racks one's focus slightly to address films of the Second World War, a similar unevenness in national film production prompts questions about how the war shaped ideas about homeland and freedom. In the United States a government-sponsored film program emerged in the late 1930s that sponsored documentary films associated with the benefits of Roosevelt's New Deal, the massive program of government investment and employment created to offset the devastations of rampant unregulated finance and the Great Depression. When the U.S. entered the war, Pare Lorentz and his documentaries of rural life ceded the film department to Hollywood types recruited to explain to Americans "why we fight." Frank Capra's seven-part series of that name, shown to every recruit in the armed forces, enlisted everything from Disney animation to clips of Nazi film to Soviet spy footage in order to generate a plain picture of the enemy for American soldiers. In Britain the government-sponsored documentary unit, the Crown Film Office, also continued to produce documentaries in the tradition begun by the lionized director John Grierson in the 1930s, but the British films, by contrast, paint a picture of the home front, stolid and pragmatically "taking it" while also exuberantly alive and civil. In Humphrey Jennings' beautifully poetic film *Listen to Britain* (1942) a carefully mixed asynchronous soundtrack animates a series of images of civility amidst the bombing, of pleasure amidst the hardship, of nature and industry in tandem withstanding the challenges put to Britain by the Axis. Capped off by a piano recital by pianist Myra Hess in the fortified National Gallery, the film cultivates the British spirit, democratizing taste across class and region, and it further showcases an appreciation for Jewish talent in the face of the enemy's hatred. Even the British "re-enactment" film about Royal Air Force bombings in Germany, *Target for Tonight* (1941), lays heavier emphasis on the jovial contributions of the Scottish navigator MacPherson ("Mac") than on the horrific risks of the bombing missions and the (admittedly later) annihilation of cities on the ground. By studying films comparatively across an epoch, one does not have to make recourse to the generalities of "national character" in order to see extraordinary variation in national-popular discourse as it seeks to enlist the support of the people for war.

Listen to Britain, like its Griersonian precursor *Song of Ceylon* (1934), also experiments with the atmospheric and evocative powers of sound. Both films precede British experiments in recording natural sound from speaking subjects *without* the use of scripts on location (these were to wait until after the war), yet both occupy prominent places as examples of experimentation in the use of sound in cinema. An alternative history, then, exists as a string of technological innovations in cinema, whereby we speak of the "silent period," or the "coming of sound," or the development of Technicolor, or the invention of Dolby surround sound. While film historians chart seismic shifts in the aesthetic and industrial organizations of cinema following significant innovations, they also demonstrate how changes in technology neither precisely precede nor simply follow upon what appear to be ancillary effects. Instead, the imbrication of technological development, aesthetic norms, and industrial organization achieve heightened visibility at moments of dramatic change.

In the history of cinematic technology, we have but one *Ur*-example in the twentieth century: the coming of sound in the period of the mid-1920s to mid-1930s. (The other candidate might be color, but "color" films were common during the silent era, when makers hand-tinted particular frames or elements within the frame, and the use of color by the late 1930s did not, and still does not, persist in all domains of filmmaking. By contrast, sound changed everything.)

> Western Electric emphasized the connection between sound pictures and its older electroacoustic technologies by proclaiming the new technology "a product of the Telephone." RCA similarly designated its sound films as "Radio Pictures" to highlight their connection to its own electroacoustic products of the past. But the transition to sound in the movies was strikingly abrupt, and it focused people's attention in a way that these earlier technologies had not. The celebratory and intense competition surrounding the different systems led listeners to listen more closely than ever before. Audiences critically consumed these new products as they developed "the listening habit" as an important new element of their "modern life" (E. Thompson 2002: 247).

To be sure, Edison and other early filmmakers dreamt of adding sound to moving pictures; in fact, Edison's early conception of the Kinetograph reversed the priority, adding images as accompaniment to the sounds of his earlier invention, the phonograph. And it's also true that the "silent" cinema, as we have seen, rarely was: pianists and sound effects operators shaped sounds and scores to fit the images on offer in early theaters and nickelodeons, melding later into larger musical ensembles to accompany ever-longer films. As small storefront theaters and nickelodeons yielded to large downtown theaters, or "dream palaces," organs grand enough to fill the house required players who could follow the cue sheets or play scores composed especially for the increasingly long feature-length films of the late teens and roaring 1920s. The idea of sound alongside film convinced spectators; inventors needed to surmount immense technological and aesthetic obstacles to widespread and cost-effective recording of cinematic sound.

As film historian David Cook notes, "the introduction of sound is analogous in almost every respect to the invention of cinema itself" (Cook 2004: 221). For both, the technological principles predated their combination into a workable apparatus for several decades; the apparatus initially provided the means for novelty and commercial exploitation with little regard for aesthetic goals; and there existed a long temporal lag between the introduction of a workable and sophisticated machine and the commensurate elegant artistic deployment of that machine. The apparatus for sound cinema that eventually emerged followed a series of fascinating questions and debates, elevated to the status of high drama given the corporate mergers and investments at stake in its development on the threshold of the Depression. Should sound be recorded as it had been since Edison, on cylinders or more commonly discs to accompany strips of film, or should it be recorded optically directly on film? How would it be possible to amplify sound in theaters designed for silent cinema? Would the opulent movie palaces collapse if local theaters could compete with sound offerings? What aural grammar would best accompany the visual conventions of various national cinemas? How would actors trained in the exaggerated gestures and pantomime of silent cinema fare when they had to speak? To sing? And what to do about the loud hum that the actual sound cameras themselves produced on the set?

In the United States, early "talkies," such as the famous Al Jolson vehicle *The Jazz Singer* (Alan Crosland, 1927), show all the marks of their birth at a time when the technology remained aesthetically untested. That loud hum made by the cameras demanded that boxes be built around them to quarantine the sound from the set. A camera once mobile and free to roam, therefore, now rarely inched in any direction (they could neither tilt nor track), resulting in static and stilted cinematography for several years until that problem was solved with blimps (casings that muffled the sound) or, later, with quieter self-insulating camera motors. For a period of time actors, too, froze, commanded as they were to speak their lines directly into microphones – hidden in potted plants and other props – with limited range. Various methods for moving cameras, for supporting better directional microphones on booms, and for solving problems associated with synchronizing sound during the editing process eventually allowed the cinema of the mid-1930s to reap the benefits of the coming of sound, ultimately giving rise, for example, to the abstract choreographies of Busby Berkeley in his large-scale musicals, or to the use of sound to haunt characters or enhance suspense, as in Alfred Hitchcock's experiments with the film he originally shot as silent, *Blackmail* (1929).

But sound transformed other dimensions of cinema more dramatically. Most important, cinema tied itself to specific languages, with consequences for which audiences a given film could therefore reach and with both commercial and ideological ramifications. Where the intertitles of the silent cinema translated easily and cheaply from one language to another (and frequently had little actually to do with the proffered images and lip move-ments!), actors delivered spoken dialogue in a single stubborn tongue. In some cases, exhibitors compensated (and still do) simply by turning down the dialogue in spoken scenes while providing simultaneous translation. In some cases, directors overcame the problem of translation (the problem, that is, of limiting their markets for film export) by recording a film simultaneously in two or more languages. *Der Blaue Angel* showcased the talents of Marlene Dietrich, who performed a German-language version as well as an English-language version, as did Greta Garbo in her first talkie, *Anna Christie*. More commonly, dubbing replaced the orig-inal language with a second language, mixing sometimes more, sometimes less seamlessly with the music and effects to create a new soundtrack. Finally, subtitles, used as early as 1907, achieved the status of preferred technique for preserving the original text and intent by the 1929 screening of *The Jazz Singer* (Egoyan and Balfour 2004: 22). The coming of sound, then, freed some national cinemas to surmount the linguistic barrier through indigenous production, while it also allowed Hollywood to adapt to long-held hegemonies in Spanish- and Portuguese-speaking markets, for example, by producing feature-length films in those languages and, later, by dubbing and subtitling its products into those languages. At present, cinema's speech poses far-reaching questions about the "foreignness" of film, about the problems of recalcitrant monolingualism and xenophobia, about the possibilities of what film can offer via "'subtitled images' . . . that extend, rather than preclude, the possibility of relating to others" (Egoyan and Balfour 2004: 22).

The coming of sound as a history of technological innovation, then, reveals the need to expand models of film history to encompass broader frames, international contexts, competing paradigms. It is not simply the case that film has become "global." It has always been so, and from its earliest years; what we mean by calling it "global" is actually quite complicatedly to do with our consciousness of and approach to *globalization*. But it is true that the interdependence of production resources, markets, audiences, and communities means that film historians need porous and pliable models for understanding these dependencies and connections, including their aesthetic and political consequences. Likewise, periodization more generally helps to package a messy past into the orderly rhythm of a semester, but it, too, immediately reveals the difficulty of understanding industrial / economic, social, intellectual, aesthetic, technological, and ideological dimensions of cinema simultaneously. An important rubric that has sought to capture that simultaneity is the idea of national cinema, to which I now turn by way of four case studies.

NATIONAL CINEMAS

By virtue of its spoken language and its stories, as well as by virtue of its ties to commercial and legal structures, cinema can be characterized as national. Regardless of where a film was shot and edited (and under what laws of union or non-union labor), and regardless of the nationality of its stars or director, some country or other stamps its seal of approval and / or its registration of copyright on the film print, and off a film leaps into the labyrinths of (usually) international distribution and exhibition. Multiple people from various places conceive of and produce a film, multiple legal systems sustain a film during its life, multiple corporate entities with homes from Delaware to Grand Cayman nourish its growth, and multiple audiences (regional, national, air travelers, DVD pirates) greet it on its travels, but we may speak with some coherence of a national cinema insofar as we refer to that ensemble of political / legal and industrial / technological configurations that provide for a film its *provenance*. The examples that follow help to clarify this.

HAMMER HORROR

British popular culture of the mid-twentieth century was no exception to the dominant trend of Americanization, and the phenomenon was not a new one. As early as 1927, responding to the flood particularly of American films across the Atlantic, the British Parliament passed the Cinematograph Act, "aimed at protecting and encouraging British film production" (Landy 1991: 244). By setting aside a quota for the exhibition in British theaters of indigenously produced films, Parliament invited a number of shoddy films dubbed "quota quickies" into Britain's theaters. Not all genre films of the post-war period conform to this category, however, given the extent to which the British film industry sought to rebuild itself in the aftermath of wartime conflicts precisely by addressing social and cultural concerns, not specific entirely to Britain but shared and generated in these complicated years. As Landy observes,

> The films of the postwar period, too, are a fruitful source for examining profound contradictions in the public sphere, contradictions which expose fundamental tensions in the public and private spheres and work against the grain of efforts to recover traditional values. The focus on family melodramas and social problem films is indicative of the social and cultural displacements of political concerns onto the terrain of family life. The horror and science fiction films further reveal pervasive sexual and social conflicts.
>
> (Landy 1991: 14)

In her study of the Hammer horror films of the 1950s and 1960s, Landy further observes the necessity, as I've suggested in the introduction to this chapter, of a dynamic view of history and the complicated relationship film bears to its context of emergence. If one begins with an assumption "that representation is a heterogeneous locus of official and unofficial articulations, of public and private desires and their prohibition, of conformity and resistance to conformity, then the horror genre, like other genres, is expressive of social life and its contradictions" (Landy 1991: 389).

What characterizes Hammer films? Quality, low-budget filmmaking, culminating in a series of searing horror films (Terence Fisher's *The Curse of Frankenstein* [1957] or his *Dracula* [1958]), in which British gothic melodrama met Eastmancolor with resounding success (see Figure 3.1). The company itself was small, shaped by powerful figures in (get it?) *Hammer*smith: theater-owner Enrique Carreras (whose son James and grandson Michael followed) and William Hinds, owner of a jewelry shop group (who also performed in amateur variety shows under the pseudonym Will *Hammer*, and whose own son, Anthony Hinds, was also to follow). The story of the company's success comes in the relationship between the initial producing entity, Hammer Productions, and a separate distribution entity, Exclusive Films, Ltd. To fulfill the demand for quota films, Hammer Film Productions, Ltd. registered as a separate entity in 1949. Taken as a group, the B-films of Hammer / Exclusive until the 1950s covered every major niche of demand from its chain of theaters: drama, documentary, comedy. But thematically, as scholar Jim Leach suggests, the most productive accounts of the Hammer phenomenon "stress the tension between restraint and excess" (Leach 2004: 170).

In the early 1950s, Hammer / Exclusive began US co-productions with Robert Lippert, whose company was subsumed into 20th Century Fox in 1955. That year's successful release of *The Quatermass Xperiment* catalyzed the conglomerate's movement into horror films previously made successful by Universal. Directed by Val Guest, *The Quatermass Xperiment*, after the play-cum-franchise by Nigel Kneale, concerns the becoming-monster of the lone survivor of the crash of a rocket that had been sent into orbit by a rationalist scientist. If playwright Kneale torqued the theological and philosophical tensions between morality / theology and rationalism / scientific method, Guest's adaptation, like the Hammer horror films to follow, shocked its audiences with a prolonged sense of the disruption of social existence, with the zone of breakdown, with the decomposition

Figure 3.1: *The Brides of Dracula.*
Source: Hammer/Universal/The Kobal Collection.

of meaning and signification. Within a few yards of this wandering, tortured, desperate, boundary-less, inexpressible existence, Hammer's *Quatermass* dispenses with most of Freud, the idea of liminality, theories of sadism, and most academic or arcane interpretive work on the psyche more generally! Audiences understood the portrait more commonsensically: from this representation derives an extraordinary power of occupying a world in-between. It is not so much that one might want to read this monstrosity as specifically British (or as specifically American, since the film was co-produced), but that one might notice how this monster takes shape within genealogies of Anglo-British contexts: the British origins of gothic fiction, the enduring links between monstrosity and reproduction, the anxieties about scientific experimentation in the 1950s following atomic devastation, optimism regarding scientific breakthroughs and space travel. Folded throughout these contexts is an overarching sense of conflict between modes of knowledge, between tradition and the dramatic changes science brings to shared, communal life. This is not so much a theme but an enduring tension in both the British and the American mid-century. Hammer's hits after *Quatermass* revel in Eastmancolor terror and sensationalism, but they, like the earlier film, press at polarities of worldview and social conflict, revealing significant points of contact with a public as eager for terror and dripping blood as for dramatization of the monstrous character of a rapidly changing world.

NIGERIAN VIDEO FILMS

The Nigerian video film functions as a form of national-popular culture in the face of dramatic changes, too. Begun in the 1970s, the film industry now produces over 1000 films (initially videos, now VCDs [video compact discs]) per year, both in Lagos and in northern Nigeria. Both in Nigeria and in the Nigerian diaspora, the films stimulate vital debate and conversation about the issues they raise, resulting in what Onookome Okome describes as a "popular public" (Okome 2004: 5). An astonishingly profitable and versatile industry centered in Lagos responds quickly to contemporary issues, to the stories, everyday habits, and themes of African people, and insofar as this cinema shapes social life through the recreation of social events, it functions less as a forum than as a force for national culture. The critical challenge involves reformulating histories of response to African cinema both as an organ of "third cinema" and as a vanguardist art cinema distributed largely through festivals such as the premier African film festival, FESPACO (Le Festival Panafricain du Cinéma et de la Télévision de

Ouagadougou), held in Burkina Faso. The Nigerian video film industry, in other words, outpaces critical response to its new aesthetics and to its new modes of industrial organization.

As with other national cinemas, the borders leak. Audiences for the Nigerian video films are scattered throughout Africa, Europe, and the Americas. But even within the country, the films write or rewrite the geographies of postcoloniality. The city film, a genre dealing specifically with the ambivalent promises of migration to the city, functions as a flashpoint for the tension between the shiny surfaces of commodities and the pull of tradition, the pleasures of emancipation and the daily struggles of survival in precarious economies. Other genres such as the religious film, and the subset of these known as the "hallelujah video film," set traditional forms of spirituality against the redemptive forces of Christianity. Whether explicitly evangelical – screened in churches and in religious convention grounds rather than in those video parlors that bring small audiences together – or linked to familial and social conflicts, these English-language films, like soap operas, function as sites for transcoding the public and the private spheres through which the nation is constituted.

Video films emerged in the context of traditions of the popular arts in Nigeria, foremost among them strands of Yoruba performance, including the *alarinjo* art, which morphed from masquerade ritual (bearing some similarity to the Italian *commedia dell'arte* of the sixteenth century) into a modern Yoruba popular theater in the mid-twentieth century. If the video films follow from this tradition, they do so in two ways: in their strong ties to audiences and in the generic mobility the industry displays. Where previous films by the Senegalese directors I have mentioned, such as Ousmane Sembene or Djibril Diop Mambety, arose from art-based practices (training in film schools, distribution by embassies and on festival circuits), the aesthetically "cheap and cheerful" as well as plentiful video films found instant audiences, creating stars and star directors just as quickly. Outside the dominant distribution and exhibition structures, the circuits in which the video films travel resemble the emerging circuits of global media more than the limited public spheres of art-based cinema practices modeled on European cinephilia.

In terms of genre, the video films move, as well, from films focused on those rituals such as witchcraft that appeal to popular audiences, to the city films, to comedies and so on. If they capitalize on success, responding nimbly to audience tastes and also to commonsense conceptions of the world, they mutate in ways that dominant critical approaches find it difficult to appreciate. They borrow from available models, grafting B-movie sensationalism onto the kinds of indigenous traditions represented by *alarinjo* art. Topics or themes of the films include ritual / religious cults and secret practices, corruption and class conflict, religious fundamentalism, the dangers of wealth, forms of transmutation such as human-to-animal, and the like.

Okome demonstrates how centrally these films address women: "at the core of video narratives is the female subject – the woman of the home and of the street" (Okome 2004: 5). And women form the core of the audience for the films, at the same time lacking any central role in their production or in the industry more broadly. The paradoxical position of women in the video film, then, offers an occasion to understand how images of women *in* the films shape and produce conceptions of femininity and roles for women who *watch* or consume them. Okome's reading of the two-part film *Glamour Girls* (1992 and 1994) explores the uncritical treatment of women in the sex trade in the city and the extent to which the films engaged in the "reaffirmation of social events by dramatizing what is already experienced" (Okome 2004: 8):

> The narrative intervention into the stories of the glamour girls [women in the sex trade who deal with rich businessmen and politicians] is patronizing in many ways. The story is told from a patronizing view that sees the action of the glamour girls as something coming from fickle minds. It re-enforces the patronizing attitude employed by male video filmmakers in matters dealing with the explosion of a social problem such as prostitution in the city. By producing a second part of the story of the glamour girls, the producer indirectly tells us that the first part of the story was a success with the audience and that he is in constant touch with the drift in society. Local newspapers in Nigeria have "wept over" the theme of prostitution in the second part of this film as soon after it was discovered that some Nigerians go to Europe just for the purpose of doing prostitution.
>
> (Okome 2004: 8)

This dramatization of the already-known suggests the films' conservative function, solidifying attitudes and positions rather than challenging them or provoking change. Yet to dismiss the industry *in toto* is to miss the chance to understand how it produces and also circulates ambivalent or contradictory responses to a rapidly changing world, a world that is, moreover, remapped through the transnational routes the films themselves sketch as they leave Nigeria for broader audiences. Tunde Kelani's hit film *Thunderbolt* (2001) is as easy to see as any Harry Potter film; it's cheaper to buy and a better challenge for the student of cinema who might delve into its issues of Igbo and regional affinities and popular discourses with the verve of a Hogwarts scholar whose eye is cast not nostalgically onto the colonial past but outward toward a postcolonial world.

SPAGHETTI WESTERNS

If the Nigerian video film creates a world of its own through its fusion of themes and genres as well as through its transnational circulation, the Italian or spaghetti western – which had its heyday in the 1960s and 1970s – combined the ingredients of the western genre into quite a different yet strangely autonomous world of *its* own. Like the British horror films and Nigerian video films, too, the spaghetti western emerged out of rapidly changing transnational industrial forms of organization, giving rise to a free-for-all competition for audiences and film markets against the increasing dominance of television by the 1970s. If "Nigeria" stretches beyond its national borders in terms of ideas about the world that the video film conveys and redresses, a coherent sense of the nation "Italy" standing behind the Italian westerns is even more difficult to discern. In fact, casting aside the curtain is more likely to reveal some version of "America," a phantom always conjured in the cataclysms of violent expansionism at the heart of the western.

The popularity of the western is directly attributable, in fact, to the extent to which American film and television had by the 1960s saturated world markets. The origins of the genre lie in the historical experiences of the American frontier, to be sure, and the details of a distinctly American everyday life (from Stetsons, to dishes of beans, to horses and covered wagons) combine with what Edward Buscombe calls the "imaginative geography" (Buscombe 1988: 17) of the western frontier to yield an iconography and topography instantly recognizable as American. But if the narrative forms derive from the dime novels of the nineteenth century and the elaborations of the frontier developed by James Fennimore Cooper (whose romantic boundary, after all, is to be found in upstate New York), the cinema's affinity with physicality, particularly the deliciously spectacular possibilities inherent in violent confrontations, makes the American foundations of the western available to other distilled versions of frontier conflict. The spaghetti westerns build upon the central tension Cooper elaborated: the savage but free wilderness (woods, desert, range) vs. the domesticated or refined but confining settlement (town, outpost, home). Yet they do so not by leaving America entirely for the Spanish locations of Almeria (where Sergio Leone shot these early "Italian" films), but by preserving a question about America's *dominance*.

European and Asian film industries could not help but respond to the dominance and subsequent decline of American film in the post-war period. While American films flooded markets directly following the devastation of national film infrastructures in the Second World War, these national markets rose from the ashes just as television began to eat at Hollywood's power in the 1950s. Reeling from the *Paramount* decision in 1948 – the Supreme Court decision effectively dismantling the American industry's monopolies in the form of vertically integrated companies combining production facilities, distribution networks, and theater chains for exhibition – the Hollywood studios flailed or collapsed as they sought to reform themselves in accordance with American law. Among the victims were the independent studios distinguished by the production of B-westerns: in the year 1953, for example, there were ninety-two westerns produced in Hollywood; ten years later, a mere eleven (Buscombe 1988: 48).

In the face of Hollywood's decline, the genre of the western found new life in international co-productions, a name for a wide variety of corporate and geographical shufflings that allowed for innovative cross-national financing, production, and, to put it broadly, imaginative possibilities. Two adaptations suggested themselves as models: the translation of Japanese art-cinema director

Akira Kurosawa's masterpiece *The Seven Samurai* into the American western *The Magnificent Seven* (1960) and the German adaptation of Karl May's novel *Der Schatz im Silbersee* (1962). In terms of thematics, the former highlighted the appeal of the mercenary, the hired elite, whose ethical and physical life provoked questions and immediate response; and the latter provided a blueprint for pragmatics, for the importation of a minor American star in a relatively inexpensive production shot in Europe to appeal to European audiences.

In Buscombe's analysis, the continuities between American westerns and spaghetti westerns reveal themselves through the presence of American actors and through the adaptation of American themes pushed to their limits by their Italian interpretation. Lex Barker, the American actor who had formerly played Tarzan and found himself starring in *Der Schatz im Silbersee*, inaugurated a movement across the Atlantic that continued with Eli Wallach (who played the bandit chief in *The Magnificent Seven* and later played Tuco / The Ugly in *The Good, The Bad, and The Ugly*); and, of course, Clint Eastwood's career in the spaghetti western elevated an American television player to international stardom. His role in *Per un pugno di dollari / A Fistful of Dollars* (based on yet another Kurosawa film, *Yojimbo*) launched a string of Italian hits, with Eastwood developing with director Sergio Leone a new grammar of cinematic action.

Leone, the reigning king of the spaghetti western, adapted American themes of mercenary justice into heightened meditations on human existence and forms of dependency. His worlds of men – for there are very few women in the genre – collide with one another in bursts of violent anger, and they also co-exist with one another in interludes of silent homosociality, accompanied by the scores of legendary film composer Ennio Morricone, with whom Leone frequently collaborated. Rod Steiger and James Coburn star together in *Giù la testa / Fistful of Dynamite / Duck, You Sucker* (1971), an oft-derided film that exemplifies the fluid treatment of Americanism in the genre. In this Italian production shot in Spain with American and British actors, an IRA bomber ("Sean / John") joins a Mexican bandit ("Juan") in the ideological maelstrom of the Mexican Revolution. Says a stripped American passenger on a wagon robbed by Juan early in the film, "You'll pay for this! I'm a citizen of the United States of America!" Juan's father responds, speaking for the genre to America, "To me you are a naked son of a bitch."

In *Fistful of Dynamite* as well as in the cycle of films starring Eastwood, Leone crafts a double-edged comment on America (see Figure 3.2). Through the films' style, Leone replicates the spectacular elements of Hollywood as "dream factory." Morricone's scores are operatic, combining hoofbeats, whistles, voices, and rhythms into textures that intertwine with Leone's extravagant images in widescreen format. Stylistically, Leone's westerns admire everything that America, and particularly American film, represents. Thematically, however, Leone's attitude explodes that same dream. Cynicism is the order of the day, violence the only option for action, the dollar the sole currency of human value. In the era of Vietnam and the Kennedy assassinations, Leone gives voice to longstanding ambivalence (following at the very least from the American occupation of Italy following the Second World War) about Americans in Europe and about Americanization of the culture industries at large. So, too, does he offer a provocative commentary on what it means to be Italian, what the history of that country's unification has meant to the precarious political settlements of the post-fascist era, and what role the country might play in the aftermath of similar political settlements following the uprisings of the 1960s.

BOLLYWOOD

Juan's little gang of bandits might represent this minor genre of the Italian western nipping at the heels of a still-enormous American film industry. Yet despite the extent to which Americanization remains a persistent force in the world of cinema, the Indian film industry remains the world's largest and provides for millions on the subcontinent and in the Indian diasporas a touchstone for national definition. As Ashish Rajadhyaksha explains,

> In its scale and pervasiveness, film has borne, often unconsciously, several large burdens, such as the provision of influential paradigms for notions of "Indianness," "collectivity" (in the generation of an unprecedented, nationwide, mass-audience), and key terms of reference for the

Figure 3.2: A Fistful of Dynamite.
Source: Rafran/San Marco/The Kobal Collection.

prevailing cultural hegemony. In India, the cinema as apparatus and as industry has spearheaded the development of a culture of indigenous capitalism "from below," and its achievement in doing so continues to influence and determine newer programming and publishing strategies with the proliferation of television channels and mass-circulation fan magazines.

(Rajadhyaksha and Willemen 1994: 10)

The phenomenon Rajadhyaksha dubs "gigantomania" (Rajadhyaksha and Willemen 1994: 10) – the sheer scope of Indian film production – refers primarily to the mainstream Hindi film industry dubbed Bollywood (again, a neologism for Bombay Hollywood). The "Hindi film" describes the song-and-dance formula film in color made since the 1960s not only in Hindi, or in a colloquial combination of Hindi and Urdu known as Hindustani, but also, with variations, in over a dozen regional languages; the issue of language is political, not only in terms of regionalism but in terms of the ostensible "neutrality" of Hindustani. Telling the story of the emergence of the Indian nation-state following independence in 1947, these romantic musicals and melodramas followed from Mehboob Khan's *Mother India* (1957) and are characterized by spectacle, excess, and hyperstylization.

While some histories of Indian cinema emphasize the differences between Bollywood and the dominant mode of Hollywood narrative cinema, these accounts tend to re-center Western and Hollywood cinema against presumed "alternative" forms when in fact these forms are themselves dominant across much of Asia, say, and they furthermore deserve to be studied alongside other modes of cultural production of Indian cinema. In his book *The Ideology of the Hindi Film* M. Madhava Prasad in fact argues that, since the Bollywood films congeal out of heterogeneous production streams "of manufacture in which the whole is assembled from parts produced separately by specialists" (Prasad 1998: 31–2), it should come as no surprise that they depart stylistically from norms sedimented in Hollywood. And the Bollywood industry can be productively understood alongside the other cinemas of India, for the Indian cinema as a whole comprises, in addition to these Bollywood spectacles, "parallel" and regional film practices.

Born in the 1930s, a cinema of social protest grew from three main companies: Prabhat, Bombay Talkies, and New Theatres. Bombay Talkies in particular nurtured India's first megastars in Devika Rani, Raj Kapoor, and Ashok Kumar, while New Theatres found success with P.C. Barua's *Devdas* (1935), first made in Bengali then remade in Hindi with K.L. Saigal as the leading man. The version in Hindi spawned an enormous following, and the film was lavishly remade in Bollywood in 2002. The seeds of India's parallel cinema were sown in these companies. Nourished by the influence of Italian neorealism following upon the Second World War, a new cinema began to take shape in the 1950s, with the release of Satyajit Ray's landmark film *Pather Panchali*, the first installment in his "Apu" trilogy. Ray's compatriots, if sometimes lively challengers, in the state-sponsored "New Indian Cinema" of the 1960s and onward included fellow Bengali directors Ritwik Ghatak and Mrinal Sen, both of whom also energetically contested the mainstream cinema (which, in turn, just as energetically condemned their products).

This New Indian Cinema was an inadequate umbrella designation for a number of different aesthetic and ideological projects, differentiated still further by regional and linguistic differences. In a country with more than twenty officially recognized languages, regionalism has been and remains structurally important to India's film industries. Centers of film production exist for the Kannada (Karnataka State) film industry, the Tamil film industry, and the Telugu film industry, and there are also notable productions in Kerala and Malayalam. While the influence of the New Indian Cinema may thus continue to be felt in the art-house cinema and on Doordarshan (Indian television), the *avant-garde* or "New Wave" changed in the 1980s and 1990s in conversation with an evolving Hindi mainstream cinema. The 1994 film *Bandit Queen*, for example, takes realism to extraordinary new places with its portrait of a low-caste woman who became a real-life Robin Hood heroine in northern India. The film explicitly indicts Indian sexism and caste discrimination and takes a horrifyingly direct look at one woman's exploitation and degradation (see Figure 3.3).

The mainstream cinema, on the other hand, preserves its interest in formulaic entertainment, sharing some standard and enduring features. The films run longer in duration than those of many national cinemas: at roughly three hours, they require an intermission. And they generally combine a variety of generic elements. While many are love stories or action pictures, they all incorporate song-and-dance routines, some used fluidly to drive the narrative while others punctuate the narrative in more staccato rhythms. The industry employs professional "playback" singers for the songs, while the onscreen actors and actresses lip-sync and perform the dances; the musical numbers therefore have more autonomy than do many of their counterparts in other cinemas (and play on their

Figure 3.3: *Bandit Queen*.
Source: Kaleidoscope/Arrow/The Kobal Collection.

own as music videos on television programs, for example). Bollywood recycles, adapts, translates, and otherwise incorporates diverse material into its stories, remaking Hollywood films, remixing or reinterpreting its own successes, and responding to increased interest from spectators around the world to its products.

BOX 3.1: SUMMARY

What these examples mean to suggest is that *all* national cinemas recycle, adapt, translate, and otherwise incorporate elements from other sources. To speak meaningfully about the history of film and the role cinema plays as and in history, we must nonetheless invoke those places and peoples of the cinema in specific and delineated ways. If periodization often strangles anomalies into patterns, it ought to be tested and pushed and otherwise questioned even as it may prove useful in making the archive manageable. Likewise, if the litany of technological change partakes of a kind of determinism, wherein all change is attributed to a single cause, it ought to be probed and similarly questioned rather than taken as objective science or as *fait accompli*. (Emily Thompson's ongoing work, for example, challenges the truism that the systems for recording sound on disc were uniformly seen as unwieldy and difficult to manipulate.) Finally, if the study of national cinemas keeps alive the dynamic relationships between state and industry, between industry and culture, between makers and their audiences, and between audiences and critical perspectives, we may generate understandings of those stories and images coming to us from Bosnia and Iran, from South Korea and Chile, and from Nottingham and Nebraska more thoroughly, more vibrantly, more powerfully. In Chapters 4 and 5, then, I turn to other models for the understanding and study of cinema more generally, models for the study first of production and exhibition and second of reception.

4

THE PRODUCTION AND EXHIBITION OF FILM

Here we move to some nuts and bolts of how films are made and exhibited in different contexts, from artisanal to industrial, from amateur to professional. Again, a word about the chapter's organization is in order. While "production," "distribution," "exhibition," and "reception" all constitute major arenas for the study of cinema, these sectors belong to differing orders of description, depending upon both the origin of the explanation and the scale of the undertaking. "Production," "distribution," and "exhibition" chart, for example, the three major arms of the *industrial* cinema as described both by the people who work in them and the academics who study them; studios, distribution companies, and theaters correspond to the material structures these arenas designate. In the case of large-scale industrial film **production**, a highly differentiated workforce with a hierarchical and strict division of labor contributes specialized elements: read the astonishingly long list of credits of a blockbuster next time you're in a theater. In talking about **distribution**, we generally refer to the labyrinths through which films move from producer (filmmaker, studio) to exhibitor (theater). And in talking about **exhibition**, we differentiate the organization and practice of showing films (issues ranging from theater acoustics to projectionist unions) from the practices and habits of **reception**, of watching or making sense of them. To survey the field of production thus understood (and the massive efforts of publicity coordinated to distribute inordinately expensive films successfully), one needs some understanding of its key jobs and functions, learning (finally!) what a **key grip** or **Foley artist** does, and through what mechanisms their labor combines into the final product. To survey the fields of distribution and exhibition within this industrial context, one needs some understanding of how tightly the corporate knot that binds them has been historically tied, and how synergies function within global technologies and entertainment behemoths.

"Production," loosely speaking, might refer equally to the acts of imagining, shooting, and editing a one-minute film-school project. In this sense, production distinguishes one *process* from another. By that logic, one might talk colloquially about the process of making movies, followed by the process of watching (or responding to or analyzing) movies, no matter the scale or the mode of production. With the prospect of the commercial universal release (simultaneous theatrical and DVD release) finally upon us with Steven Soderbergh's *Bubble* (2006), the ever-narrowing "distribution window" (that distance between theater and home viewing) collapses (Risen 2005: 62). Not that the practices of distribution or exhibition have ever been stable or unitary. From embassies to art houses, from pirated DVDs to cheap VCDs, from production-financing deals for European television rights to tie-in campaigns with McDonalds; the realm of making movies depends entirely on the circuits they will travel once "in the can." Even the fate of your one-minute three-point lighting exercise depends upon recruiting an audience willing to cheer you on.

That process of production understood in broad terms, moreover, generally shakes out into three, whatever the context: pre-production, production, and post-production The chapter's first section, "Making movies," explains who does what in each of these, where you might learn to do various tasks, what it takes to make a 16mm film or digital film, and how film production is organized technically and economically. The second section, "Studying film production," then introduces the reader to some of the many issues tackled by film studies scholars who focus on production: industrial modes and centers of production and their ideological effects, labor issues, the institution of stardom, genre studies (focusing on those genres you have already encountered, including westerns, melodramas, musicals, horror films, and crime films), film censorship, authorship, technological innovation, the role of the state in film production, and the realm of art film (schools, festivals, museum exhibitions). The third section, "Contexts for studying production," takes three examples to illustrate how scholars generate and treat the problematics that emerge from production. In that section I look at cinema practices marginalized by academia such as gay porn; analyses of genre and ways of thinking beyond genre; and, third, the ways in which distribution can function as authorship. A brief and final note, "Studying film exhibition," links the practices of film production to the practices of film exhibition, examining in particular the building of a mass audience. From film trains and Hale's tours, through vaudeville and nickelodeons, to movie palaces and suburban multiplexes, exhibition practices shape audiences and our conceptions of how spectators engage with films produced under many different models.

MAKING MOVIES

Anyone can make a film. Experimental filmmaker Maya Deren knew it was possible to do so on the cheap as early as the 1940s:

> Cameras do not make films; film-makers make films. Improve your films not by adding more equipment and personnel but by using what you have to the fullest capacity. The most important part of your equipment is yourself: your mobile body, your imaginative mind, and your freedom to use both.
>
> (Renan 1967: 41)

With the independent film sector exploding in past years, it becomes increasingly imaginable for any given person with a good idea, more frequently a bad one, to undertake a film project. In the United States, Michael Moore's pit-bullish documentary *Fahrenheit 9/11* (2004) and the cult breakout Mormon-inflected narrative film *Napoleon Dynamite* (Jared Hess, 2004) both cost less than a half-million dollars to make. Jonathan Caouette's autobiographical film *Tarnation* (2003), about his relationship with his mentally ill mother, edited at home on his laptop, reputedly cost $218 (although later editing and music clearances pushed the cost of the film in distribution up to $400,000) (Ramsey 2005: 13). The young Thai director Apichatpong Weerasethakul, whose alluring and inscrutable surfaces in films such as *Sud Sanaeha / Blissfully Yours* (2002) or *Sud Pralad / Tropical Malady* (2004) I recommend pursuing on your own, makes feature films that circulate on the world festival circuit as well as on inexpensive DVDs released initially in Thailand. Another exciting young director, Argentinian Lucrécia Martel, attracted the attention of the Spanish filmmaking genius Pédro Almodóvar, who is helping to draw attention to her two outstanding features, *La Ciénega* (2001) and *The Holy Girl* (2004), on the global circuit. Armed with the knowledge of film language and film history such as you've learnt, you would be ready to enter the first phase of filmmaking: pre-production. This is followed – logically enough – by production and post-production, and together these three steps describe the process of making movies at whatever scale, from artisanal solo efforts at home or on the soccer field, through larger yet still modest productions such as Moore's with location shooting and a sizeable crew, to extravagant studio productions with the imprimaturs of *Kong* or big-name directors in Japan or New Zealand or South Africa. (Incidentally, Lillian Ross' on-set account of the making of *The Red Badge of Courage*, in her fifty-year-old book *Picture*, remains at the top of my list of books about studio productions.)

Pre-production involves the elaboration of an idea from inchoate premise to a plan for movie-making and includes all the tasks one must complete before actually shooting a film. In the case of a small-scale film, pre-production begins with elaborating an idea over several written stages. A proposal sketches the idea in a nutshell, whether it's a focus for a documentary (follow eight kids through a spelling competition), an experimental film (put one camera on the Empire State Building for eight hours), or a narrative film (tell the story of the 1919 "Black Sox" scandal, when the Chicago White Sox baseball team threw the World Series). (These proposals incidentally evolved into *Spellbound* (Jeffrey Blitz, 2002), *Empire* (Andy Warhol, 1964), and *Eight Men Out* (John Sayles, 1988), respectively.) A proposal evolves into a more elaborate version, still a nascent idea, called a "**treatment**," in which, for a narrative film, the characters but especially the structure and logic become clearer; a treatment explains how plot advances, how dramatic action unfolds,

BOX 4.1: *GRAND ILLUSION* (RENOIR, 1937) AND *RULES OF THE GAME* (RENOIR, 1939)

Early treatments capture the core of a film's idea. Here are the opening scenes from Jean Renoir's great films *Grand Illusion* and *Rules of the Game*, introducing the essence of his interest in social relations and in the idea, as François Truffaut quotes Renoir, that people "are more divided horizontally than vertically" (Truffaut, quoted in Bazin 1997: 172). Characters and props already define the protagonists.

GRAND ILLUSION: 1916. BEHIND THE FRENCH LINES.

> In an air corps canteen we find the career officer Stanislas de Boïeldieu, a cavalry captain. Monocle in place, riding crop in hand, with a touch of arrogance and impertinence. He asks a pilot to take him on a reconnaissance flight. It is Captain Maréchal, a rugged character, without polish, a mechanic by trade. The fortunes of war and his own merits have brought him his commission very quickly. Boïeldieu and Maréchal are of the same rank, but not of the same world.
>
> (Renoir, quoted in Bazin 1997: 172–3)

And here is *Rules of the Game,* the scene that becomes the opening greeting at the airport:

PROLOGUE. THE PARIS OPÉRA.

> A great concert is being given by Paul Stiller. It was his friend Robert Monteux who convinced the great conductor to come to Paris and who financed this sensational performance. Monteux is very proud, and he accepts the congratulations as if he had composed the music himself. Great enthusiasm from the audience. Monteux decides to follow up this triumph by asking for the hand of Christine, Stiller's daughter.
>
> Conversation between Christine and André Cartier, a flyer. André Cartier loves Christine, but he loves flying even more, and the young girl feels unable to enter into a world so foreign to her.

She assists her father, and by marrying Monteux, a prominent antique collector but also a patron of music, she will not have to change her activities. Only one person is not enthusiastic about the marriage. It is Octave, forty-five years old, a friend of Stiller's for the past twenty-five years, and unsuccessful musicographer, who knows Christine like a daughter, having often stayed at Stiller's in Vienna, more or less sponging off him. He likes Monteux, but he likes Christine more, and he thinks that the newly-weds will not get along with each other for long because Christine is more intelligent and Monteux, despite all the money he has earned, is a fool. People make fun of him. But the marriage is set.

SCENE I. AT THE AIRPORT.

The "Marseillaise" fills the air and the crowd is enthusiastic. André Cartier has just landed, having smashed all the world aviation records.   Description of the kind of insanity that takes possession of a euphoric crowd.

The most eminent public figures congratulate Cartier. The most beautiful women throw kisses to him. Finally he manages to reach his car. It is a beautiful automobile in which his chauffeur whisks him away. To get back to Paris he will have to take an extensive detour since the heavy traffic has blocked the direct route.

(Renoir, quoted in Bazin 1997: 187–8)

and how characters function in terms of that structure. (Even an avowedly *avant-garde* premise can benefit from some form of sketching or elaboration.) From proposal to treatment, from treatment to script or **screenplay**: a screenplay follows a common format and supplies full dialogue between characters, the locations of every numbered scene, and all of the action in the story.

Formatting the screenplay according to a standardized protocol allows everyone who might be involved with the production of a narrative to understand every scene's components and demands. Popular software packages such as Final Draft or Sophocles permit simple manipulations of the screenplay's basic ingredients. First, to make it possible to identify a scene during shooting, each scene is numbered. Because each page of a screenplay occupies roughly one minute of screen time, knowing the page count of a given scene is crucial. Following each scene number comes the location, either interior (INT) or exterior (EXT) of that scene's action. When planning a day's shoot, a director most frequently collects a group of scenes that can be shot at the same location (as opposed to shooting the scenes sequentially). Characters' names appear initially in bold face, so that readers can track the appearance of new characters and assemble the appropriate actors to shoot each scene, and all dialogue appears in the middle of the page, making it simple to assess which characters have speaking parts in a given scene. Finally, sounds or sound effects appear in capital letters, providing preliminary cues about how the film will eventually sound. From screenplay to shooting script: this expanded version of the screenplay adds all of the information necessary to transform the screenplay into actual images and sounds. To realize the film, every shot, every camera setup, and every movement is planned in advance in the shooting script and often in **storyboards**, sketches of every shot which suggest further visual information about each shot's realization, from scale to proportion, to angle, to screen direction. While some directors rely more heavily than others upon storyboards in pre-production planning, the work of pre-production maximizes the chances of making a good film in the end.

Subsequent stages of pre-production follow from having a screenplay or a developed film property, and whoever is ultimately responsible for financing the film must give it a "go" or a "green light" before it enters the next phases of pre-production planning. These include **casting** (of principal actors, extras, stunt doubles and the like, either through an agency or casting director or by choosing your friends wisely), location scouting (choosing locations for shooting), research (into ship-to-shore communications or seventeenth-century Vienna or the electrical components of robots or whatever your subject), **production design** (generating the overall "look" of the film through the art director's supervision of set design, décor, and illustration, as well as costume design), set construction, and costume (and our beloved hair) design. All of these activities must, furthermore, adhere to a strict budget, administered and supervised by a **line producer**, so called because the

BOX 4.2: *ALMOST FAMOUS* (CROWE, 2000)

The scene from Cameron Crowe's semi-autobiographical film *Almost Famous* preceding Russell Hammond's introduction to Penny Lane reveals volumes about the rock and roll scene through beautifully condensed humor:

Int – Backstage steps – Night – Minutes later.

PENNY: I found you a pass.
WILLIAM: *(amped, distracted)* Thanks. I got in with Stillwater.
(*as he writes*)
The guitarist, Russell Hammond, he just thoroughly opened up. He is by far the best and most honest interview I've ever done. (*she nods*) I've only done *two*, but you know. He's *number one.*
PENNY: You're learning. They're much more fun on the way up.

William nods, still scribbling. She eases down into place on the step next to him. Her proximity causes him to look at her, his eyebrows rising. She smooths them down with two single fingers.

How old are you?
WILLIAM: Eighteen.
PENNY: Me too. (*beat*) How old are you really?
WILLIAM: Seventeen.
PENNY: Me too.
WILLLIAM: Actually I'm sixteen.
PENNY: Me too. Isn't it *funny?* The truth just *sounds* different.
WILLIAM: (*confesses*) I'm fifteen.
PENNY: You want to know how old I really am?
WILLIAM: (*immediately*) No.

She looks upstairs, soaking in the sound of another band tuning up. Music is her religion.

(Crowe 2000: 39–40)

budget divides along a line containing "above the line" costs of story rights, scenario, producer, director, cast, and fringe benefits; and "below the line" costs of just about everything else, including extras, staff, art and set costs, light platform, labor and materials,

effects and miniatures, and the like. The production budget determines all that will follow in the next phase.

The **production** phase technically encompasses, for a feature film,
only the activity of **principal photography**, that is, the shooting and
sound recording of the principal performers and the essential
actions. But even principal photography enlists the services of a
small army of talented laborers. Captured by the first unit of
production, the director, and principal actors, the principal photography is the meat of the film, supplemented by the work of the
second unit, which contributes inserts, backgrounds, aerial photography, special location shots, action sequences, and the like. For a
smaller production, various combinations of technical expertise in
crews draw from these general structures.

Overseeing the production team, the director's job, as Bruce
Kawin explains it in his excellent overview of filmmaking in *How
Movies Work*, is "to arrange and direct the action, to indicate where
the camera ought to be, and to decide which takes ought to be used
in preference to others" (Kawin 1992: 363). Assisting the director, a
crew of five involves itself closely in decision-making on set and,
perhaps most crucial, in tracking what actually gets from script to
film. The first and second assistant directors (A.D.) form a chain
from the director's ultimate responsibility downward, with the
second A.D. responsible for crowds and for buffering the production
from the public. Formerly known as the "script girl," the **script
supervisor** keeps track of what is to be shot (and what sound
recorded) in each scene as well as what is actually shot; the supervisor times the script, anticipating the final length of the assembled
film, and records detailed notes to assist the director in moving
from scene to scene. For those viewers who avidly note mistakes in
continuity (a character is bare-headed when leaving the house, but
miraculously appears with a beret in the exterior shot), the script
supervisor may well be your culprit to blame. Assisting the script
supervisor, the dialogue director tracks changes in dialogue from
rehearsal, where actors often forge new approaches to the script or
tweak its details, to what makes its way to the take. And finally, the
cuer, who works with cue cards and teleprompters if they are to be
used, rounds out the director's crew.

Directors work closely, of course, with actors, primarily with
those principal actors (often called lead actors) or stars, and, as we

know, not every lead actor is a star. In terms of how commercial feature films structure authorship, several actors' names appear "above the title," in a credit sequence added during post-production. A product of contracts that link the intellectual property to its realization in the film product, credit sequences generally open with the name of the studio, then list the production company, then list the investment group, then list the director's first credit, then the stars' names, then the title of the film. The director's second credit nudges as close as possible to the film text, but the stars' preeminence signals their cut, their importance to this film's allure, and their future profitability based upon how this property fares. Other actors appear further down the hierarchy: character actors, whose fame derives from the ability to play certain types with success or finesse, bit players, who have small credited parts, and, at the bottom of the pile, extras, who appear uncredited in crowds or backgrounds.

Actors of all types depend for their livelihoods upon those who give them their filmic allure: the cinematographer and camera crew. For unionized labor in large-scale industrial undertakings, accreditation from an organization such as the American Society of Cinematographers functions as much as a badge of professionalism as a method of receiving due protection and compensation. In the United States, the cinematographer or director of photography (D.P., or in the UK, DOP) generally chooses cameras, film stock, lenses, filters, and other equipment in close consort with the lighting designer and crew. In Britain, the lighting cameraman handles the lighting, while the director works with the operative cameraman to control the camera and action. The lighting designer collaborates with the cinematographer to achieve the two cardinal imperatives of image-making: balance (control of the tonal range from black to white, dark to light) and consistency (balance from shot to shot). If in small productions a cinematographer controls all elements of the camera and lighting, in larger productions a camera crew supports the D.P. on set: four cameramen (first, second, first assistant, and second assistant) and a still photographer deal with everything from following focus through loading film stock to slating takes and taking production stills to use in publicity. Frequently the cinematographer sits at the director's side to watch **rushes** or **dailies**, those takes recorded during each day of shooting, to evaluate what needs to be re-shot.

Sound crews similarly record all elements of production sound, usually divided into the categories of sync sound (recorded in synchronization with the camera) and wild sound (not synchronized), both of which belong to the category of live sound, recorded during shooting (as opposed to post-production). The production sound crew assists with **booms** for microphones (operated by the sound assistant or, predictably, the boom operator) and affixing smaller microphones on set. Later the sound crew, led by a production mixer, combines a preliminary sound mix, much of which changes in the post-production phase, when our **Foley artist** steps in to perform replacement sound effects, from footsteps through squealing tires to raindrops dancing on tin roofs.

Rounding off the production team, a gaggle (bevy? flock?) of managers attempt to control the chaos of principal photography. In addition, a film publicist stokes interest in the production in the trade press, leaking bits of the story or tales of the production to maintain interest until the film's carefully calculated **release date**. While lawyers enter largely at the post-production phase, accountants keep the production on budget and adjust it only when absolutely necessary. A transportation and catering crew attend to the needs of hungry hoards at constantly changing locations, while prop(erty) masters and animal trainers contain the things, furry and otherwise, necessary at each location for each scene. Finally, there is also a mysteriously named crew responsible for electricity, and a crew responsible for moving and hauling work together on set. The **gaffer** is the set's key electrician, his assistant the **best boy**. The **key grip** is the supervisor of the grips, who do the physical work of setting up dollies and cranes, laying tracks for dollies, controlling camera cables, and the like.

As these physical labors of filmmaking yield to touches of buttons, and as analog film yields to digital media, increasingly films are actually made in the post-production phase, a world rapidly changing due to the constant invention of software used for digital effects or computer-generated imagery. When editing on film, laboratories process various optical effects such as titles, fades, dissolves, wipes, blow-ups, skip frames, bluescreen, compositing, and double exposures, all of which now form part of the post-production work of digital processing. (Laboratories still play a vital role in the entire process, correcting exposure and light levels at every stage of printing, calibrating quality of release prints on different gauges of film, and so on.) This post-production world opens new possibilities for further effects, including cel animation (a type of animation using layers of plastic sheets called cels, which are then stacked on top of one another to form the complete image), scale modeling and miniatures, claymation, digital compositing, animatronics, use of prosthetic make-up, morphing, and various forms of computer-generated graphics and imagery dependent upon code software developers write every day.

Post-production on complicated narrative feature films combines the labors of additional armies of technicians and artists, enlisting whole studios to create models and miniatures, others to develop prosthetics and computer-generated humans complete with muscles and hair. Effects teams work with others in post-production, notably the editing and sound personnel, including music composers and editors as well as sound editors and compositors. If editors determine shot length, selection (from many takes of a given shot), and sequence, sound editors must combine hundreds of different tracks of sound (including dialogue, music, and noise) into mixes to accompany the edited images. Gunfire doesn't convince without the cracks of rifles; murder doesn't make sense without dramatic context.

In the past decade, major films such as *The Matrix* (1999), with its special bullet effects, and the *Lord of the Rings* trilogy (2001–3), with its motion-capturing techniques, invent and refine new techniques of spectacular image-making. The Disney film *Dinosaur* (2000) and the DreamWorks / Pacific Data Images film *Shrek* (2001) pushed computer animation to new levels of realism (with the liquid and fire effects in the latter, and with the fusion of live-action photography with computer-generated Disney animation in the former). But "realism" (or "accuracy" or "authenticity") is never simply the goal (and in the case of *Shrek* the effects were scaled away from realism to create a more "cartoony" look). Whether working with rotoscoped images (such as those in *Waking Life* [2001]), with kung fu moves, with carefully choreographed fights or with claymation (or Plasticene animation) figures, new effects serve the same masters as in previous decades. They command attention, they attract audiences, they generate "oohs" and "ahhs," but most of all they generate profits.

STUDYING FILM PRODUCTION

To learn more about the economy of cinema and also about the ways in which films speak to audiences, film scholars turn to the industry less with an eye on its internal machines of innovation (although those fascinate many of us) and more with a sense of evolving institutions that generate particular problematics (or ways of generating useful questions) for analysis. While many scholars generate textual analyses, the most compelling studies of cinema situate those readings within other rubrics, juggling aesthetic, social, psychological, and other balls simultaneously. **Stardom**, for example, is one rubric that no doubt has changed from the days of Florence Lawrence, whom you met in Chapter 1. Studios and large-scale industrial cinemas across the globe manufacture stars, yet their social functions and types change over time. Cycles of innovation and co-optation or stasis define **genres**, as you have seen with horror or the western. Japanese horror films constitute a genre now within a tradition arguably begun with Hammer, and westerns, as you also now know, give us glimpses of ranges from Mexico to Spain to Africa. Authorship requires redefinition in an era when indie productions vie for screen time with megaproductions involving thousands in cast and crew. Censorship shifts in response to patterns of self-regulation (such as the moralistic Production Code – that system of self-regulation adopted by the Hollywood studios under pressure primarily from Catholic organizations in the 1930s) and overt state regulation (in the case of ownership restrictions and anti-monopoly legislation), while many film industries operate under guidelines, more or less well elaborated, of self-censorship or self-regulation. Various forms of technological development shape new possibilities for cinema, as we know from the history of film, but so too do various forms of organization of production itself, from industrial through post-industrial (and classical to "post-classical" Hollywood style) to artisanal (and "indie") and entrepreneurial. Finally, a crucial question about film production derives from cinema's role as social institution with ties, if precarious ones, with pillars of public life: museums, festivals, churches, political organizations, and similar public fora all foster and circulate certain kinds of films, overlapping in some measure with "art" film, political film, and new media. Film scholars who are above all concerned to investigate the image of ourselves that cinema refracts, at particular moments and places, turn to these arenas of cinematic practice for explanation and provocation.

While it would be futile to condense each of these into a page or two, let me turn to several examples (to do, in order of their appearance, with stardom, extensions of genre, and distribution practices) of how film studies scholars fruitfully approach questions of production. These foreground the extent to which models of intellectual analysis respond to changing assumptions about the field of film studies as well as changing practices of filmmaking around the world. They also inspire me with their intellectual clarity, rigor, and capacity to spawn many lines of inquiry.

CONTEXTS FOR STUDYING PRODUCTION

STARS

The star of studying stars (at least in Anglophone film studies circles) is Richard Dyer, a British scholar who published his first book on stardom, *Stars*, in 1980 and who has registered important updates and revisions ever since. He helped, significantly, to pinpoint the social definition and function of stars. While filmgoers and critics hailed and booed lead actors from the early days of cinema, that is, and while actors in small budget and non-commercial films may display oodles of talent, stars properly belong to the peculiar alchemy of large-scale commercial movie-making combined with mass audiences: stardom is a social institution, Dyer makes clear, rather than a property of an individual actor. Audiences, in a strong sense, produce stars in tandem with the apparatuses of filmmaking. Central to the latter are the triple engines of star production, promotion (the activity of the makers in putting a star and a film in the minds of the public), and publicity (the activity of others, including the press, in attending to that star and film), together yielding another odd creature, the star's *persona*. Not quite the star's own *personality* (for that we rarely access, particularly in an unmediated fashion), not quite the star's *image* (for that resides in photographs and films of him or her), not quite the star's *character* in any given film or star *vehicle* (for that would constitute but one iteration of what contributes to the persona), and not quite *the sum of a star's roles* over time (for other elements of the star's behavior – like a nasty drug habit or an illicit affair – are crucial ingredients, too); the star persona draws from all of these realms and is constantly recalibrated to address changes within any or all of them. If John Belton's basic definition of a star holds – "a performer in a particular medium whose figure enters into subsidiary forms of circulation, and then feeds back into future performances," his secondary emphasis is even more important, that the star-image is always both incoherent and complete (Belton, quoted in Braudy and Cohen 2004: 598–9). Dyer's initial stable of stars – Marlon Brando, Bette Davis, Marlene Dietrich, Jane Fonda, Greta Garbo, Marilyn Monroe, Robert Redford, and John Wayne – belonged to a group most interesting, then, for the contradictions and tensions that obtained between differing elements of their personae. In the cases of Dietrich and Garbo, sexual ambiguity and what we might now call queer overtones overwhelmed versions of femininity seemingly beloved of 1930s Hollywood. In the case of Fonda (at a certain moment well before the debacle that is *Monster in Law* [2005]!), her political commitment to ending the war in Vietnam and her embrace of roles emphasizing female agency such as in *Klute* (1971) reshaped a persona founded upon the sexpot image of just several years earlier in films such as *Barbarella* (1968) (see Figure 4.1).

In Dyer's later writings queer resonances of star-images come to the fore, and he concentrates on some forms of cinema at once more recalcitrant and more marginalized than those in the belly of the beast that is Hollywood in its so-called golden age. In *The Culture of Queers*, he offers a spectacular close analysis of the gay pornography films, for example, of a star called Ryan Idol, "a young man who must have blessed his parents and perhaps God that he was born with so appropriate and serviceable a name," quips Dyer (Dyer 2002: 193). Observing the extent to which gay porn obeys many of the same conventions as classical Hollywood, although perhaps pushing them to breaking point, Dyer finds the pivotal formal element (as well as source of excitement) of the films of Idol in gay porn's tension between illusionism and performance, yielding a particularly dense type of self-reflexivity. Keying into the instability that obtains in the relationship between the fact of being a movie star and the character a star plays, Dyer extends his investigation of the social reference inherent in star personae through the case of Ryan Idol.

Figure 4.1: Barbarella.
Source: Paramount/The Kobal Collection.

The conclusion Dyer draws from his analysis surprises, and it is this conclusion that propels the analysis of stardom into new galaxies: contrary to the long-held supposition that artistic work that draws attention to itself (self-reflexive art) has a distancing effect, the "viscerally demanding" genre of gay porn, like much gay culture, nonetheless draws us *in* (Dyer 2002: 201). Building upon the insights of queer theory, Dyer finds that "performance in the Ryan Idol case means much more display, presentation, artistry, the commitment to entertainment – literally a good show. It is a construction of sexuality as performance, as something you enact rather than express" (Dyer 2002: 202). Bringing the study of stardom from his early studies in *Gays and Film* (1984) to the present, Dyer hones in exemplary fashion theoretical tools alongside close readings in order to push longstanding questions having to do with realism, pleasure, and stardom into new and more fruitful formulations.

GENRE

Genre, too, is subject to such reformulation; indeed, the *idea* of genre is premised upon iteration and repetition with a difference. Commercial film genres such as the western and the musical, whether in Arizona or Andalucía, Hollywood or Bollywood, depend for their lifeblood upon ever-new variations on a prescribed pattern. They garner the interest of critics frequently when they, like pornography, become reflexive, as in Peter Wollen's admiration for *Singin' in the Rain* (1952) (Wollen 1992). Classical Hollywood musicals may, as Jane Feuer argues, be congenitally reflexive, insofar as they are shows about putting on shows:

> What makes the musical unique among film genres is not so much that its heyday neatly coincides with the studio years, but rather that its reflexive capability rendered it that genre whose explicit function was to glorify American entertainment while at the same time being itself a form of entertainment (as were all genre films).
>
> (Feuer 1982: 90)

Other genres, such as the road movie, seem to do self-critique better than they do self-reflexivity. *Thelma and Louise* (1991) generated as much commentary about its generic intervention as about its portrait of feminist rage. As Steven Cohan and Ina Rae Hark read it,

> Its female couple, who replace the male buddies or heterosexual lovers of earlier road movies, react to the failure of patriarchy to support their

desires, just as the register, the dynamic interaction of character and its road setting, identify their fantasies with their means of escape (Louise's green Thunderbird convertible) and, most of all, interrogate and, to some critics, overturn the masculinist bias of the road.

(Cohan and Hark 1997: 11)

But genre, as you will now have gathered, is a slippery way to characterize different types of film that rely for their common heritage less on formula than on a moment or, alternatively, on a worldview. I'm thinking, in the case of the former, of Italian neorealism or of *film noir*, both of which emerged quite specifically *as categories of production* in relation to the cataclysmic events of the Second World War, and, although some of their stylistic elements find repetition to the present day, both of them refer to bounded bodies of work. I'm thinking, in the case of the latter, of both melodrama and of ethnographic films. While melodrama may refer equally to the "woman's film" of the American 1940s and Mikio Naruse's Japanese *shomin-geki* (movies about the poor and lower-middle classes), such as *When a Woman Ascends the Stairs* (1960), melodrama broadly speaking suggests a way of conceiving of the theatrical nature of lived experience, a fondness for didacticism and heightened codes of expression and bursts of affect, and an attention to psychological conflicts expressive of social relations that remain submerged or unexpressed. Ethnographic cinema, too, might be understood as a way of conceiving of the world through a representational practice, like the "Orientalism," well studied by Edward Said, that compulsively objectifies indigenous peoples (Said 1978).

Film scholar Fatimah Tobing Rony in fact sets ethnography as a practice of racializing people against history as a process of universalizing them. Against definitions of ethnographic film that stress its mediating capacity across different cultures, or its reflexive practices gesturing toward a modernist aesthetic sensibility, Rony uses the term "'ethnographic cinema' to describe the broad and variegated field of cinema which situates indigenous peoples in a displaced temporal realm" (Rony 1996: 8). And while it may appear that such a definition disregards the specific conditions under which different fields of cinema – such as art films, scientific research films, educational films used in schools, colonial propaganda films, and commercial entertainment films – come into being, the opposite proves true. By *not* assuming that each film *a priori* serves the master of an ideal of mediation or critique of realism, Rony can attend to the actual mechanisms of racialization in a given instance of filmmaking practice.

A controversial example of ethnographic cinema, as elaborated in Rony's terms, is the epic Robert Flaherty film *Nanook of the North* (1922), considered widely to be the first feature-length documentary film, the first ethnographic film, even the first art film (see Figure 4.2). (It was, in fact, a commercial film, distributed by a French studio, financed alongside trading expeditions.) *Nanook* famously documents the struggles of an Itivinuit (indigenous northern Canadian) family against the vicissitudes of nature, following "Nanook, the hunter," and his clan through a harsh winter, from the "civilization" of the trading post into the temporary shelters of igloos in the apparently isolated tundra. It is a film of extraordinary beauty, in awe of the landscape it confronts, and clearly delighted by moments of interaction with Nanook and his people. Many critics herald Flaherty's film as an achievement in Romanticism, insofar as he captures the very essence of humanity:

Figure 4.2: Nanook of the North.
Source: Flaherty/The Kobal Collection.

"Family life, the human condition, are conquests from which animals are excluded. Such, in essence, is the theme of the film. Nanook, the hero of the first ethnographic film, is also the symbol of all civilization" (De Heusch, quoted in Rony 1996: 100).

In Rony's reading, however, *Nanook* is better understood as taxidermy, that practice which tries to make the dead look as though it were alive. Flaherty, on this view, resuscitates a dying culture – dying, it must be added or emphasized, at the hand of explorer / filmmakers such as Flaherty – as a "cinema of archetypal moments endlessly repeated," constituting in sum the myth of the first man (Rony 1996: 102). Her reading does not elide those remarkable aesthetic accomplishments for which the film continues to garner praise: the long takes, the sense of landscape, the use of reframing, and the like. Through Flaherty's myth and mythmaking cinematography, she suggests, indigenous peoples are thus relegated outside of history proper through a number of tropes Flaherty solidifies over the course of the film: they are associated with raw meat, their bodies are preserved as spectacles, their forms of response are seen as naïve, their limited contact with the West renders that contact amusing and benign, and so on. But Rony also takes a step beyond a reading of the text of the film to situate it within a broader discursive world, which is to say that she visits social ideas about Inuit cultures alongside what the Inuit themselves had to say about Flaherty and the film (no one even thought to ask them about it until the 1970s). The result is a strong critique of the idea of participant observation, the kind of ethnography Flaherty thought he was practicing: Rony ultimately is interested in how ethnographic spectacle solidifies boundaries between Primitive and Modern, representation and reality, precisely by appealing to the idea that audiences *thought they were watching "authentic" anthropology*. No matter that "Nanook" was named Allakariallak ("Nanook seemed to suit the whites better," commented a descendant of one of Flaherty's Inuit friends" [Rony 1996: 123]). No matter that the "family" Flaherty assembled for Nanook contained Flaherty's own Inuit common-law wife. According to Rony, and to be tested by your own reading, what Flaherty assembled through his own self-fashioning as the Great Explorer and participant observer is a sustained taxidermy of a culture that had already been lost for years before Flaherty arrived on the scene, only to be reconstructed toward "ethnographic" ends.

DISTRIBUTION

If Dyer reads stardom through the prism of formal analysis combined with queer theory, and if Rony reads genre backward through an overarching ideological argument about the function of "ethnographic spectacle," what framework emerges for thinking about what may seem a mundane aspect of cinema, that is, distribution? Can distribution as an object for study, in other words, be intellectually exciting or provocative? Justin Wyatt, an American scholar turned industry executive, shows us just how powerfully a distributor shaped a film text with his reading of the British and subsequent American release of the 1992 film by Irish director Neil Jordan, *The Crying Game*.

In the case of this successful American release, the conundrum of authorship comes from the studio's rewriting of the film in its marketing campaign for its American audience, an audience that receives it differently than its initial audiences. Film scholars have argued successfully, in other words, that the version of *The Crying Game* seen in the United States was actually a different film than that seen by audiences elsewhere. The film's distributor in the United States is of course none other than the behemoth Oscar-chaser Miramax, an independent "minimajor" in the year of the film's release, poised for dramatic absorption by Disney in the subsequent year. In order to understand the contours of authorship at this moment, then, it is helpful to see how industrial structures mutate to accommodate diverse production, distribution, exhibition, marketing, and advertising methods that determine the marketplace for independent film. In order to develop movies able to break out of niche or art house markets, both New Line Cinema and Miramax, the two largest independent film companies at this moment, conceived of the film package in different ways. Wyatt suggests that while "New Line has continually favoured gradual expansion and diversification only following breakthrough successes, Miramax's presence is based much more on marketing and targeting audiences beyond a narrow art house niche" (Wyatt 1998: 76). Such was the strategy for *The Crying Game*.

A romantic thriller that reworks the themes of Jordan's earlier film *Mona Lisa* (1986), *The Crying Game* centers on a story of a man's search for his identity. In the first half of the film, Fergus

(Stephen Rea), a member of the IRA, kidnaps Jody, a British soldier (Forest Whitaker), with the help of seductress Jude (Miranda Richardson) while Jody is on leave at a carnival outside of Belfast. Kept in captivity by a group of IRA operatives, Jody looks for friendship and sympathy to Fergus, who is increasingly drawn to his prisoner and who learns through their interchange of Jody's "special friend" Dil at home in London. When Fergus receives the order to shoot Jody, the plan is botched when Jody runs, Fergus is unable to shoot him in the back, and the British army invades the IRA hideout at the same moment. In the second half of the film, Fergus escapes to London, loses himself in an alias ("Jimmy" from Scotland), seeks out Dil, and strikes up a relationship with her, only to be found out by his former IRA associates, who enlist him in an assassination scheme. By the end of the film, Dil has shot Jude, and Fergus pays for her crime in jail.

This summary, of course, omits the very detail around which the film's advertising campaign in the United States was built: the fact that Dil is transgendered. "This major secret," Wyatt observes, "was responsible for the film's cross-over success; due to the barrage of publicity and press coverage growing from the secret, an amazing $62.5 million was grossed by this film which would seem to be firmly within the boundaries of the art cinema" (Wyatt 1998: 81). In their book *The Film Experience* (2004), Timothy Corrigan and Patricia White use the film as a case study for readers to examine precisely these shifting contexts of promotion and the ways in which a film's promotion shapes audience's responses and readings:

> [E]specially in the United States, word of mouth functioned as the most powerful strategy in the promotion of *The Crying Game*. Viewers, including most movie reviewers, were urged to keep the secret of Dil's sexuality as a way of baiting new audiences to see the film. A widely announced word-of-mouth promotion – 'Don't tell the secret!' – drew a continuous stream of audiences wanting to participate in this game of secrets. Word of mouth became part of a strategy to entice American audiences who, anticipating a sexual drama of surprises and reversals, would in most instances overlook the political tensions that complicated the film for British audiences.
>
> (Corrigan and White 2004: 29)

By way of corroborating evidence, Corrigan and White cite the poster campaigns in Britain and the United States, in which, in the former, Stephen Rea's portrait is combined with a smoking gun to promote the film's political violence and the tag lines emphasize Jordan's authorial legacy ("daring film," "brilliant," "Jordan's best work to date"), whereas the American poster features only the image of Miranda Richardson with a smoking gun and three key words: "sex, murder, betrayal." The phrase "play at your own risk" follows the film title on the poster, while Jordan's directorial reputation is subordinated to the generic appeal of the thriller, in which "nothing is what it seems to be." Miramax, in other words, functions as an auteur in this year in its role as distributor, cutting the film's political references and enlisting audiences to take up the generic elements of intrigue.

What is useful about Wyatt's and Corrigan and White's emphasis on promotion in this case study is that it alerts us to the circulation of films in context, rather than to the more circumscribed task of producing hermetic textual analyses. British and Irish audiences would be aware of escalating IRA activities and the fact that an IRA bomb exploded that year in the Baltic Exchange in the City of London, killing several and injuring almost one hundred people. American audiences, on the other hand, were more steeped in the sexual and identity politics of HIV / AIDS activism and protest, in the direct actions of the group Queer Nation, and in the public demands for visibility for gay and lesbian people. American readings thus emphasized the dialectic of hiding and revelation that resonated with queer identities. Different publics produce different readings; the evident differences in the promotional campaigns capitalize upon those differences to direct attention to these divergent strains of the film's narrative.

STUDYING FILM EXHIBITION

The final example of *The Crying Game* suggests that films can be "produced" retrospectively, i.e. that practices of distribution cue audiences to emphasize elements of a film's narrative, thereby "writing" the film backwards. If this is the case, and Wyatt and Corrigan and White mount convincing cases, the exhibition of film might exert the same power to shape a film's reception (the topic of the entire Chapter 5). Before moving to complicated theories of reception and the practices of spectators and audiences, I linger just for a moment here on film exhibition as an arena that best offers us an understanding of the popular and mass audiences that preoccupy scholars of reception. For it is the singular achievement of the social institution of the cinema to have produced, over the course of its hundred-odd years, an entity shaped as much by stories and news-reels as by the architecture of theaters, the acoustic properties of speakers, the marketing practices of rogue inventors, the legacy of popular entertainments such as festivals and vaudeville and clown and puppet shows, the improvisations of projectionists, the recita-tions of the *griot* or the *benshi*, the invention of air conditioning, the culture of smoking, and the evolution of the snack concession. Exhibition practices, in other words, shape not only what we see but how we see it, and how we understand ourselves to belong to a *group* audience for movies.

I distinguish between a popular audience and a mass audience, following most scholars who think carefully about the role of cinema in society, and following in particular upon the distinctions made vigilantly and elegantly by the British Marxist scholar Raymond Williams. The idea of popular culture derives from its root *popularis*, belonging to "the people," and, according to Williams, carries with it two senses: "inferior kinds of work" (popular literature as opposed to high canonical literature, for example), as well as "work deliberately setting out to win favour," work that is well liked by many people. In this latter sense, it is most certainly not the sense of work made by the people for the people, as in folk culture or populism (R. Williams 1976: 237). In terms of a popular *audience*, then, all three meanings are possible and therefore need to be parsed: (1) an audience for the kind of work held in contempt by those who favor high culture, i.e. an audience for schlock or trash or formula fare or whatever label you choose; (2) an audience for work well liked by many, i.e. an audience credited with elevating a work by appreciating it (in this sense and in the case of a film such as *My Big Fat Greek Wedding* [2002], audiences define what is popular rather than simply consume what is already deemed admirable); and (3) an audience for work created by the people as opposed to the elites or as opposed to an industry clashing with the interests of the people / working class / peasantry. The latter valence finds expression also in the idea of the "national-popular," a formulation indebted to anti-fascist and anti-colonial struggles for national liberation, wherein cultural production is integral to the struggle for what Italian Marxist Antonio Gramsci calls hegemony or political predominance. Culture, in other words, serves to enlist support or consent for dominant ideas; the idea of culture from below, or culture produced against the needs of the dominant class, is embedded in this third sense of the popular.

The idea of *mass* culture or the mass audience is linked much more strongly to the world of consumption, but it depends, as well, upon some of the valences lodged in "the popular." As Williams notes, twentieth-century uses of the term fuse its earlier associations to create an ensemble of meanings which oscillate between contempt and valorization. With regard to "mass" media such as commercial film, one refers to "the large numbers reached (*the many-headed multitude* or *the majority of the people*); the mode adopted (*manipulative* or *popular*); the assumed taste (*vulgar* or *ordinary*); the resulting relationship (*alienated and abstract* or *a new kind of social communication*)" (R. Williams 1976: 196). Again, parsing seems necessary. First, cinema in its current mode of exhibition reaches almost unthinkable numbers of people: more people have seen James Cameron's *Titanic* (1997) – the hands-down highest-grossing film of all time – than voted in the election that resulted in the second term of George W. Bush. Visionary film-makers from Dziga Vertov and Sergei Eisenstein onward have appreciated Lenin's dictum about Bolshevik transformation: "For us, the cinema is the most important of all arts," a belief the new state embraced by creating cinema trains that exhibited revolutionary films throughout the new Soviet Union. The second sense, the mode adopted, is related insofar as "mass" refers to how cinema acts as a social force. Is it true that "there are very few original eyes and ears; the great mass see and hear as they are directed by others" (R. Williams 1976: 195)? Or might cinema act as a positive force, expressing a common purpose for many who come together in the dark? The third sense derives from our answer to these questions: does cinema then deceive its spectators into accepting social truths that run counter to their real interests, or does cinema offer a potentially transformative vision or form of communication?

The history of film exhibition helps us understand the construction of the film text as well as the film audience. If the initial viewings of Edison's films were solitary in the sense that one "peeped" into the Kinetoscope one at a time, cinema has nonetheless always been a social event mining other popular and mass arts for its own textual practices. Early exhibitions in the United States interlaced films with vaudeville and minstrel performances; early exhibitions in Taiwan inserted a short film with commentary by a *benshi* into the performance of an opera. The idea of films as integral and separate forms doesn't emerge until they are severed from their connections with other performances. Early projectionists also created their own programs, stringing films together but also splicing films according to those logics they believed would please spectators. Whatever notion we may harbor of the integrity of the film text comes later, when commercial films marketed through catalogs with plot summaries and promotional materials replace the ingenious combinatory talents of their exhibitors. Some critics focus on how, even today, texts derive their contours from their exhibition practices: Anna McCarthy shifts the critical discussion about television away from a simple opposition between the focus on private, domestic consumption and the exhibition of television in public spaces in her book *Ambient Television* (2001). In bars and in airports, television can become an occasion for community and conflict, defining its publics and the politics of public space in fascinating ways, even simply at the level of the placement of the screen.

Let us begin with the most pervasive positional convention of the TV console in public places: its placement near the ceiling of a room, secured and immobilized above eye level and out of reach of the casual user of the space. How does this positioning, in and of itself, make a statement about the space, its users, and its proprietors within a rubric of public and private? On the one hand, this overhead placement guarantees equal visual access for all viewers. It is a positioning that designates the screen as public address, perhaps even public service. Yet, on the other hand, putting the screen out of reach like this marks it as private property (McCarthy 2001: 121).

As anyone who has watched TV in public knows, what is *on* is hardly the issue: the structure of exhibition and the mental / physical / psychological state (exhausted, drunk, pretending to be waiting for someone, afraid of a diagnosis) of those of us who turn our eyes to the box affect what we see in or on it.

The history of exhibition has been at the center of recent significant debates in film studies. In a series of exchanges in *Cinema Journal*, Ben Singer, Robert Allen, and others examine the "boom" of nickelodeon theaters in Manhattan in the years between 1907 and 1909. What may seem a quantitative matter of combing archival sources for accurate information about the number and location of theaters during that period actually gives rise to a vibrant discussion about the questions and methods of historical study. At stake, first of all, is an image of a dark, dank, smelly storefront theater populated by working-class ghetto-dwellers. While this myth of early cinema exhibition dominates superficial histories of the cinema, it simultaneously obscures real questions about the class composition of early audiences and the locales in which early theaters might have been found. To what extent did theaters attract middle-class audiences or find homes in middle-class neighborhoods? What was the *role* of the middle class in relation to characterizations of the cinema's pleasures and effects? Second, in trying to answer those questions in the absence of variegated census data or reliable city records historians confront difficult questions about how to integrate secondary with primary sources, and how to raise questions that adequately respond to available data. If theaters were in particular types of neighborhoods populated with particular classes (not to mention ethnicities and races) of people, to what extent can we extrapolate from that information about the types of exhibition experiences that obtained in those theaters? In the shift from nickelodeon exhibitors to converted legitimate theaters in this period, moreover, what was the role of vaudeville, or what persisted in terms of the mix between theater and film? Finally, if historians find suitable responses to some of these questions in the case of Manhattan, what will they have learnt about exhibition in the period more generally? What, as Robert Allen asks, "can we generalize from this to the exhibition situation anywhere in the United States beyond the East and Hudson Rivers" (Allen 1996: 95)? Data from Manhattan may suggest class segregation in the movie-going experience, while the experiences of many in small towns suggest that the movies provided places, like the taverns of McCarthy's study of television, "where people of different classes met and mingled" (Allen 1996: 96).

Exhibition practices deserve far more scrutiny than this brief section prompts, but the take-home point is this: production and exhibition dynamically constitute both text and audience. The ways in which we conceive of audience have profound implications for how we understand what films are, what they mean, how they work upon us. If "reception studies" can be split off – and I don't think it can – from studies of making and showing films, Chapter 5 merely continues the discussion begun here.

BOX 4.3: SUMMARY

Film production takes place on a variety of scales, from the artisanal to the process of serial manufacture of the commercial industry. Knowing *that* labor is divided yields insight into filmmaking as a complicated and coordinated process; every move is planned and chance banished as far as possible. Knowing *how* labor is divided in the three stages of filmmaking – pre-production, production, and post-production – sheds light on that to which we usually respond as a film *text* or *experience*. Multiple drafts of a screenplay might yield evidence of a screenwriter's response to censors, for example, or storyboards that differ from the final product might suggest technical obstacles to a director's vision. To study film production is to study this massive process from its multiple angles and institutions, from labor unions to product placement to stylistic patterns to the lives of its personnel and so on. If I limit myself here to examples (of stardom, genre, and distribution), it is due to the overwhelming number of questions you will be quick to spot in this ensemble. Finally, the study of film exhibition draws both upon conceptions of audience (such as the distinction I trace between the popular and the mass) and upon conceptions of history (such as the relationship between the local and the national, for example). Both production and exhibition are shaped by reception, thus the artificiality of the chapter break here.

5

THE RECEPTION OF FILM

This chapter takes the reader to the heart of film study: the practice of watching and responding critically to film. Drawing from debates about literary reception and canon-formation, the opening section, "The best films," tackles the issue of *value*: how the institutions and discourses of film reception (box office performance, tie-ins, awards and festivals, "best" lists and fan activity) adjudicate films' worth. This section returns to ideas of film authorship and film signatures, as well as to film history, to address the phenomenon of the film review: the genre of writing on film most familiar to you. Although the film review can tell us much (who looks great, what's stupid, what's funny and what's not), it limits its task largely to evaluation rather than other forms of engagement that are the provenance of academic film studies. Assessing at the start some of the classic texts of reception studies, the second section, "Watching closely," surveys the range of approaches undertaken in film studies to examine modes of response, from the pedagogy of shot-by-shot analysis to the activities of film fandom. It revisits that first commandment of cinema, "Thou shalt deceive," in order to raise questions about how to understand and enrich the experience of watching films and to think about what it means to watch critically. From models of close

analysis to phenomenological reflection to philosophical meditation, this section means to expose the reader to a variety of likely
surprising and, I hope, stimulating ways of considering cinematic
response, in bold contrast to the model of passive entertainment
many bring, noses in the air, to commercial narrative film. The final
section, "Spectatorship as bridge," emphasizes links to categories of
production and exhibition, by examining how genre, for example, is
as much an industrial logic of production as it is a system for selection. Questions of spectatorship are also questions of political and
social commitments; this section closes with a discussion of feminist, queer, and critical race studies insofar as these discourses
catalyze further reflection on fundamental relations between
subject and object, looking and being-looked-at. Who looks? At
whom? And what are the limits of a regime of knowledge derived
from the gaze?

THE BEST FILMS

What makes a film great? What motivates those end-of-the-year
list-makers, furiously promoting and demoting various movies to
respond to new releases and changing tastes? What endures, and
what evanesces? Who decides, and why?

To open these questions is to talk about value, about how we
measure, calculate, traffic in, and otherwise depend upon an abstrac-
tion Karl Marx called "contentless and simple" but which is
nonetheless one of the most vexing issues in the study of the
cinema (Marx, quoted in Spivak 1987: 156). For to talk about great-
ness requires us to 'fess up to our criteria therefore, and to ask,
furthermore, after our motivations for list-making or, to put it in
more academic language, canon-formation.

Cinema, as you now know, remains a relatively young medium.
For that reason perhaps foremost, its most breathtaking accomplishments receive largely consensual praise. The oft-cited
perfection of deep space by Gregg Toland in Orson Welles' *Citizen
Kane* or the maintenance of deep focus in Jean Renoir's *Rules of the
Game* still wow us with their ability to enlist new techniques to
communicate enduring social concerns. Marlon Brando's extraordinary performance in *On the Waterfront* defines "Method" acting.

BOX 5.1: THE BEST FILMS

Here are the top twenty-five of the top 100 as listed by the American Film Institute:

1   *Citizen Kane* (1941)
2   *Casablanca* (1942)
3   *The Godfather* (1972)
4   *Gone with the Wind* (1939)
5   *Lawrence of Arabia* (1962)
6   *The Wizard of Oz* (1939)
7   *The Graduate* (1967)
8   *On the Waterfront* (1954)
9   *Schindler's List* (1993)
10   *Singin' in the Rain* (1952)
11   *It's a Wonderful Life* (1946)
12   *Sunset Boulevard* (1950)
13   *The Bridge on the River Kwai* (1957)
14   *Some Like It Hot* (1959)
15   *Star Wars* (1977)
16   *All About Eve* (1950)
17   *The African Queen* (1951)
18   *Psycho* (1960)
19   *Chinatown* (1974)
20   *One Flew Over the Cuckoo's Nest* (1975)
21   *The Grapes of Wrath* (1940)
22   *2001: A Space Odyssey* (1968)
23   *The Maltese Falcon* (1941)
24   *Raging Bull* (1980)
25   *E.T. The Extra-Terrestrial* (1982)

And here is the British Film Institute's top ten:

1   *The Third Man* (1949)
2   *Brief Encounter* (1945)
3   *Lawrence of Arabia* (1962)
4   *The 39 Steps* (1935)
5   *Great Expectations* (1946)
6   *Kind Hearts and Coronets* (1949)

7   *Kes* (1969)
8   *Don't Look Now* (1973)
9   *The Red Shoes* (1948)
10   *Trainspotting* (1996)

And this is the first section of the alphabetical listing of *Time* magazine critics Richard Schickel and Richard Corliss' top 100:

Aguirre: The Wrath of God (1972)
The Apu Trilogy (1955, 1956, 1959)
The Awful Truth (1937)
Baby Face (1933)
Bande à part (1964)
Barry Lyndon (1975)
Berlin Alexanderplatz (1980)
Blade Runner (1982)
Bonnie and Clyde (1967)
Brazil (1985)
Bride of Frankenstein (1935)
Camille (1936)
Casablanca (1942)
Charade (1963)
Children of Paradise (1945)
Chinatown (1974)
Chungking Express (1994)
Citizen Kane (1941)
City Lights (1931)
City of God (2002)
Closely Watched Trains (1966)
The Crime of Monsieur Lange (1936)
The Crowd (1928)

To take another example, as the character of the Little Tramp, Charlie Chaplin's penguin-like wobble and extraordinary gestures continue to inspire the best physical comedians and comediennes (from French comic actor Michel Simon to American standup genius Lily Tomlin), emulating his capacity to fuse the body and its parts with biting social commentary. From well-known works such as Kurosawa's heroic epics and Bergman's interior dramas to the more shadowed productions of Budd Boetticher (who made low-budget westerns) or the Kaurismäki brothers in Finland (who make trenchant comedies), the treasures of the cinema aren't difficult to list or to appreciate. There are thankfully enough of them in the aggregate, moreover, to last a good healthy lifetime.

Step back a moment, though, to think, first, about what motivates these observations about cinema's accomplishments and, second, about the terms of their praise. One motivation, more obvious for cinema than for canons of literature or of other arts (painting, sculpture, drawing), is profit. With the re-releases of "classic" movies on DVD, the owners of copyrights promote the "must-have" value of "top" films, "essential" to any discriminating film-lover's library. Free flattery ("you have good taste") gets them what they want most. Institutions of cinema such as national film institutes (the American Film Institute [AFI], the British Film Institute [BFI]) and professional organizations such as the Oscar-granting Academy of Motion Picture Arts and Sciences (AMPAS) support such calculations of value, issuing their own ranked lists or subsidizing the re-release of films for theatrical or home exhibition. To be sure, these organizations often broaden the canons they help to shape, touting the genius of a little-known director or helping to restore prints of lesser-known works (such as the re-release of Mikheil Kalatozishvili's 1964 film *I Am Cuba*), while scholars collude with reissuing companies by providing the cache of academic value to DVDs in the form of biographical notes, critical essays, research for "making of" featurettes, or voice-over commentaries on feature films. I love *The Bridge on the River Kwai* and thank the AFI for ranking it a surprising number 13, helping to ensure its availability and the longevity of that whistled tune on DVD for years to come.

If one incentive for canon-formation comes in the bottom line, another, however, comes from the desire to elevate cinema to the plane of value on which other arts sit. As early as 1915, the poet and critic Vachel Lindsay wrote an appreciative set of essays on the new medium, tellingly titled *The Art of the Moving Picture*. If film deserved its status as what Lindsay calls the "fourth dimension" of art, it required, by corollary, its own geniuses who would display the "human soul in action" as we see it in architecture, painting, and sculpture (Lindsay 1970 [1915]: 29). Argues Lindsay:

> Let us take for our platform this sentence: The motion picture art is a great high art, not a process of commercial manufacture. The people I hope to convince of this are (1) the great art museums of America, including the people who support them in any way, the people who give the current exhibitions there and attend them, the art-school students in the corridors below coming in on the same field; (2) the departments of English, of the history of the drama, of the practice of the drama, and the history and practice of "art" in that amazingly long list of our colleges and universities – to be found, for instance, in the World Almanac; (3) the critical and literary world generally.
>
> (Lindsay 1970: 45)

Borrowing the Romantic conception of the artist on which the current cult of artistic production is largely based, critics who sang the praises of cinema's high accomplishments found in its directors those same talented individuals yearning to capture unique, if not sublime, encounters with the world in which they found themselves as they discovered in poets and painters. As with poets and painters, film directors soon required institutions to sanction their endeavors and ensure their social status (as well as to protect their labor), hence awards ceremonies (Oscar was born May 16, 1929) and guilds (the Director's Guild of America, formerly the Screen Director's Guild, began its own awards ceremony in 1948).

Hence the ongoing practice, too, of attributing films to a single signature, that of the director. If you have seen in Chapter 4 the extent to which especially commercial narrative film requires the labors of many under this signature of one, you begin to see here how the idea of treating a modern industrial art form on the model of solitary artisanal practices starts to become entangled in webs of contradiction. (You will also astutely have noted that such attribution is a convention of academic writing on cinema, a convention this book embraces despite the contradictions.) As a convention of authorship, in which we understand the director to assume ultimate control over a film's production, the idea of the director signing a work may appear hardly objectionable. Indeed, many directors (Brakhage and Bruce Baillie, to be sure, but also Andrei Tarkovsky,

Terence Davies, Julie Dash) work in a vein one can only call "personal." Yet in practice, as I have begun to suggest, audiences *receive* films in multiple ways, based on a number of different candidates for their authorship: studio (insofar as an MGM film in the 1930s, for example, guaranteed a certain level of production values), distributor (insofar as marketing campaigns, such as that for *The Crying Game* discussed in Chapter 4, shape audiences' expectations and readings), star (insofar as Anthony Hopkins may exert the same audience pull as James Ivory), writer (often in cases of adaptation of literary classics, such as *William Shakespeare's Romeo + Juliet* [1996], *William Shakespeare's A Midsummer Night's Dream* [1999], *William Shakespeare's The Merchant of Venice* [2004] – the actual titles of the films), production personnel (such as particular FX collaborators or legendary cinematographers), and, finally, director. The collaborative nature of the cinema and, of course, its reproducibility militate against its easy consideration in the terms of previous art forms.

The *terms* in which many praise the best cinema as an art produced by individual genius directors invite critical scrutiny, too. In the genre of writing about cinema most familiar to you, the popular press movie review, you'll find those terms circulating abundantly. Superlatives rule, of course: best, greatest, fastest, most horrific, most realistic, most gripping, most provocative, funniest, and so on. If acting frequently recedes in the language of film analysis, it reigns in the genre of the review, where thick descriptions of appearance (soft blond hair, a curving upper lip, a body honed by workouts for a year) vie with assessments of plot. Thumbs point in two directions only: a film is a winner or a loser.

Here is a review in its entirety of a loser, the 2005 film *Wolf Creek*:

An initially promising horror film that turns exploitive, "Wolf Creek" fails to deliver the requisite payoff considering its leisurely pace. It bears the almost always dubious label "based on true events," and details the unfortunate fate that befalls two young British women, Liz (Cassandra Magrath) and Kristy (Kestie Morassi), visiting Australia, and the local bloke, Ben (Nathan Philips), they hook up with for a road trip across the inhospitable outback.

Writer-director Greg McLean admirably attempts to breathe some life into the genre by taking his time to get to the gore, but rather than

> yielding interesting characters it merely deflates the suspense. The ambling first half follows the trio as they make their way to isolated Wolf Creek Crater, and though the actors are appealing enough, their characters remain ciphers. It's difficult to care one way or another whether they win the lotto, get abducted by aliens or are cut to ribbons by a homicidal Samaritan.
>
> (Crust 2005: E7).

Calculating his own response according to genre conventions of the horror film, Kevin Crust's review condenses the essential evaluation into two terse paragraphs: featured actors, director, short plot summary, adherence to generic expectations, final say so. Since the press relies on the promotional junkets engineered by studios and their personnel, moreover, they tend to repeat the very language and sound bites of the press release or "exclusive" interview: several reviews may use the same phrases ("inhospitable outback"), tell the same story of on-location romances (likely fabricated by publicists), faux-bemoan costly set construction or the like. Focusing on plot, stars, and directorial intention, most popular reviews (and there are exceptions and exceptional reviewers) assume passive audiences and rarely access those elements of the cinema I have argued to be most powerful: its capacity to provoke, enlist, and stimulate our imaginations and critical engagement in acts of world-making.

WATCHING CLOSELY

Alternate accounts of reception, in some measure derived from the study of literature, emphasize more active relationships to cultural products. Against an influential view that a poem or novel offers up its meaning and frames of reference univocally and intrinsically, German scholars Wolfgang Iser and Hans Robert Jauss separately but relatedly proposed models of response to literary texts that took seriously what a reader brings – in terms of knowledge, experience, and openness – to the text. Iser's conception of a reader's "horizon of expectations," based upon what s / he knows, say, of the nineteenth-century novel or the Modernist poem, offered a helpful way of conceiving of readers' differing preparations and hopes for the literary encounter. Not all film viewers who see the sequence on the train station steps in *The Untouchables* (1987) will "get" the reference to *The Battleship Potemkin* (1925), but the film remains intelligible to those viewers at another level nonetheless; perhaps the new knowledge that the reference exists will now return the viewer to both films! Not all film viewers competently map histories of representation of the Holocaust onto Roberto Benigni's *Life Is Beautiful* (1997) or even onto Steven Spielberg's *Schindler's List* (1993), but they, too, understand that the former film provokes viewers to think about the unspeakable through comedy, while the latter poses unsettling questions about the role of the individual as sympathetic savior within a context of catastrophic and traumatic devastation and loss. For his part, Jauss develops a more complicated model of literary *history* in which reception is in fact crucial to a work's becoming-historical. "Literature and art only obtain a history that has the character of a process," he suggests, "when the succession of works is mediated not only through the producing subject but also through the consuming subject – through the interaction of author and public" (Jauss 1982: 15). Attending to that interaction is no small task.

The German school of reception theory, as it's called after Iser and Jauss, made possible a host of further investigations into the role of the reader, congealing in the Anglophone academy into a strain of literary scholarship called reader response criticism, some of whose practitioners trafficked in provocative claims about whether the "text" as a reasonably coherent object could even be said to exist (Fish 1980). Reader response criticism represents the culmination of a process, then, of transferring attention to the reader's *experience* of a text rather than the formal *structures* of a text such as you encountered them through formal analysis. For the study of popular culture, as opposed to the literary canon, scholars drew from this tradition as well as from the work of the so-called Frankfurt School, a moniker for a number of exiles from that German university who pursued philosophy and social scientific research in the United States during and after the Second World War. Characterized by a complicated pessimism about the potential of mass culture to contribute to revolutionary or meaningful social change, these exile intellectuals, such as Theodor Adorno, Herbert Marcuse, and others, nonetheless devoted themselves to understanding the appeal of radio, television, even astrology columns. These cultural artifacts interact dynamically, if nefariously, with their readers, Adorno suggests: "We assume that such publications [as astrology columns] mold some ways of their readers' thinking; yet they pretend to adjust themselves to the readers' needs, wants, wishes and demands in order to 'sell'" (Adorno 1994: 38). Even if they dismissed and derided mass culture for its deleterious effects, scholars such as Adorno rendered the study of mass culture mandatory for engaged intellectuals.

Reception studies, or those studies of film that are interested more broadly in cinema as a social institution, as we know them today take from these strains of scholarship several assumptions as axiomatic.

First, the "text" exists meaningfully *in its encounter* with its reader / spectator. This is not to say, following the proverbial story of the tree in the forest, that if a film is projected in an empty auditorium it therefore does not exist (although Hiroshi Sugimoto's series of photographs entitled "Theatres" demonstrates that what one records of that projection may be simply a sublime rectangle of white light). It is rather to emphasize the bodily (physiological), psychological, phenomenological, and hermeneutic activities of audiences as they interact with a film as essential to what they understand the text fundamentally to be. The thoughtful critic is aware of himself as responsive to a given film in all of these ways, yet careful not to take the self as the measure of all possible forms of engaging with it. He or she is careful, too, not to take the text as fully present or yielding to the critic's tools, either; Raymond Bellour's close analyses remain paradigmatic for their awareness of the elusivity, or unattainability, of the film text as such.

Second, the "text" may be high or low or in between: Bollywood films, Hong Kong action films, B-westerns, melodramas, and dated instructional films all solicit responses worthy of understanding. As with the school of reader response criticism, some scholars wedded to the study of popular culture are wont to lob exaggerated claims for its "subversive" or "progressive" potential. But careful ethnographic studies of working-class television viewers or of women who habitually read romance fiction teach us that these lowbrow texts live in fascinating worlds: where housing estates become microcosms for studying familial relations, or where the very act of reading becomes a vehicle for housewives to claim legitimacy as autonomous people with expanded knowledge of the world and the right to time for learning and imagination (Morley 1986; Radway 1984). Studies of film fandom similarly reveal extraordinary cultures of reception, in which acts of productive engagement (fan fiction, contributions to story lines, blogs, and fan sites) blur the lines between original production and derivative reception, professional makers and amateur watchers. Constance Penley's studies of *Star Trek* "slasher" fiction, in which fans rewrite the social and sexual lives of Kirk and Spock, appreciate the fans' intimacy with the series:

> There is no better critic than a fan. No one knows the object better than a fan and no one is more critical. The fan stance toward the object could even be described as tough love. The idea is to change the object while preserving it, kind of like giving a strenuous deep massage that hurts at the time but feels so good afterward.
>
> (Penley 1997: 3)

Third, scholars of film reception draw useful distinctions between the reader or spectator constructed by the text and the actual bodies who encounter it in the theater or living room. As you know from your study of film language, each shot of a film embeds a point of view (structured, again, by the placement, distance, angle, and focus of the camera in relation to what lies before it), whether that point of view is assumed to belong to one of the film's characters (in which case it is said to be subjective) or whether it functions as an omniscient "God's eye" view (objective) or whether it frees itself entirely from the realm of human sight and realist constraint (such as the shot in the opening moments of Billy Wilder's *Sunset Boulevard* (1950), in which we gaze up from the depths of a pool at our quite dead narrator and protagonist floating above). For every single shot in a film, in other words, we can ask, "From what point of view are we presumed to see?" And for every shot in every sequence, this point of view changes, even though Hollywood films will typically repeat camera positions (in an ABAB pattern) to alert spectators to small changes, grabbing us then with the shift to a new perspective in C. The grammar of continuity, furthermore, largely naturalizes these flights of vision, perspective, and subjectivity. When an actual person takes up these implied points of view, however, s / he may notice or perhaps resist one or another for various reasons. As I discuss on pp. 128–30, for example, feminist film critics raise unresolved questions about what happens when the implied spectator is a man who objectifies or fetishes the female body as an object of desire (think just for a moment about the opening sequence of Garry Marshall's *Pretty Woman* [1990]) but the actual audience, true for this film marketed as an updated Cinderella story, is largely female. How do women look at onscreen women who are offered as objects for a presumably male gaze? How should we think about gender in this relay of bodies, fantasies, desires, and gazes? Feminist film theory also emphasizes the need to differentiate further between the spectator as a theoretical construct (assumed to be the product of social and psychic processes) and the audience as a physical and sociological aggregate: it's possible, then, to hypothesize about "the female spectator" while not making "her" always correspond to actual women in the audience, allowing for models of reception to work at multiple levels, analytic and experiential.

Fourth, and finally, both the text and its audiences are assumed to be highly mediated and stratified, rather than transparent or univocal. Films, in other words, do not simply harbor messages to be decoded by audiences lucky enough to have been issued with a secret decoder ring. Likewise, audiences do become "taken in" by stories and by the larger-than-life images before them (even in the diminishing scales of the multiplex), but they, too, are not assumed to share an identical experience in so doing. While social differences poorly described by the shorthand categories of race, class, gender, and sexuality are often important in charting differences in reception, other habits, inclinations, patterns of viewing, intellectual interests, and so forth, shape reception, too. In what follows, I further outline several different approaches to studying reception in the cinema, and the chapter concludes with practices of reception studies you might further test on your own.

In order to understand how the language of film is structured, as well as how audiences come to understand and to respond to that language, one has to watch films closely. In Chapter 2's discussion of the formal elements of film, we took the shot as the unit of film composition most analogous to what the word is to language; many formal analyses of film thus begin with the analysis of a single or key shot to reveal a film's formal emphases and qualities, watching the shot unfold frame by frame from its beginning to end. Before the widespread use of video and subsequent digital formats, an analysis (or, alternatively, analyst) projector was the film geek accessory *par excellence*, permitting the projectionist to advance a film frame by

BOX 5.2: SHOT ANALYSIS

I'd recommend this exercise: choose a film you like and isolate a single shot you find strongly compelling for whatever reason. Watch it ten or fifteen times, noting every element of its *mise-en-scène* (setting, props, lighting, costume, hair, make-up, figure behavior); watch it ten or fifteen times again, noting every element of its cinematography (camera placement, angle, movement, distance, focus); watch it ten or fifteen times again, noting every element of its sound (speech, music, noise). Which elements most significantly shape the shot's appeal and role in the film more broadly? How do those elements convey meaning or serve a function in this shot? To what extent does this shot include elements that are repeated elsewhere, as motifs? What choices seem most important in this shot? What would you do differently?

frame without flicker. Now any cheap DVD player will do the trick of stilling the image, and lo, the wonders close analysis can reveal! (Here I use the terms "formal" and "close" analysis interchangeably, suggesting that both involve slow and thorough viewing of a film's formal elements, not as an end in itself but as an arsenal of evidence for further argumentation.)

Several examples of formal analysis have legendary status within film studies, and for good reason. David Bordwell's studies, including his excellent book on Eisenstein (Bordwell 2005), rely on formal analysis. With Kristin Thompson and Janet Staiger, he undertook the most comprehensive study of the emergence of the stylistic and industrial system known as the classical Hollywood cinema, a labor that relied on the close analysis of hundreds of films for the logic of their organization of time and space through *mise-en-scène* and editing (Bordwell *et al.* 1985). Likewise, Raymond Bellour's painstaking analyses of sequences from Hitchcock's films identify formal structures of alternation and repetition, dominant paradigms of textual organization and narrative. Bellour's analysis of Hitchcock's films, and in particular the Bodega Bay sequence from *The Birds*, reveals the gendered and sexual dynamics of

Figure 5.1: Alfred Hitchcock.
Source: Universal/The Kobal Collection.

Hitchcock's world, in which aggression against women becomes powerfully associated with the power to look (see Figure 5.1).

More recent formal analyses have spawned readings just as monumental as these. Peter Wollen's short book on Stanley Donen's film *Singin' in the Rain* includes a sequence analysis of the musical number of the title, in which Gene Kelly does his thing – splashin' and dancin' and twirlin' his umbrella – down a puddly cobblestone lane (see Figure 5.2). Wollen attends carefully to sound, combining reading with production history:

> In "Singin' in the Rain" [the musical number] the sound effects are caused by the rain and the pools of water. There is a background noise of the hiss of rain falling, accompanied by the squelchy sound of the taps. This eventually escalates to the gushing sound of the water spout and the louder, sploshing noise made by Kelly jumping up and down in the puddles. Holes were specially dug on the sidewalk and filled up with water (six puddles), precisely where Kelly's choreography demanded them, and a lake was dug out in the gutter of the street. In

Figure 5.2: *Singin' in the Rain.*
Source: MGM/The Kobal Collection.

fact, the whole number, which was shot out of doors on one of the permanent streets built on the studio back lot (East Side Street), demanded complex engineering to deliver the right flow of water through a series of pipes for the rain and the downspout.

(Wollen 1992: 16)

Paying further attention to the splendors of Kelly's performance within the film text as a whole, Wollen argues that his contribution to the film exceeds his role as star; in his direction and in his pieces of the film's script, the film registers as a high point of his career. Kelly's incredible bodily elasticity and range, on display, argues Wollen, nowhere more winningly than in the title sequence (even as one declares one's undying love for "Good Mornin'"), fuse two distinct traditions in the history of American dance: tap and ballet. Threading the vernacular with an appreciation for classical dance, Kelly's numbers tie the dance and musical numbers to the narrative; a close reading of the title sequence provides fuel for the argument that Kelly's own authorship of the musical and dance numbers significantly shapes the film's achievement.

In another tour de force analysis forthcoming in her book *Death Twenty-four Times a Second: Reflections on Stillness in the Moving Image*, Laura Mulvey isolates the first sequence of Douglas Sirk's 1959 melodrama remake of the 1934 film *Imitation of Life* (Mulvey 2004: 478). The film tells the story of two mothers, one white and one black, and their daughters, one white and one of mixed race who can pass for white. In its first shot, Lana Turner as Lora Meredith descends from a beach boardwalk to hunt for her daughter, Susie. As Turner makes her way down the boardwalk and steps onto the sand, Sirk positions his movie camera behind a jostling crowd, which includes a photographer letting loose a blinding flash on the throng. In the wink of an eye, indeed in a sequence of only several frames imperceptible when run at 24 fps, an African-American woman appears on the steps and disappears with the photographer's flash. In Mulvey's persuasive reading, this ghostly presence of the black woman in the film's opening encapsulates all that is to follow in the film's narrative involving Lora and Susie and Annie Johnson and her daughter Sara Jane: the black woman's capacity to be present only in subservience or as whiteness, never onscreen in fullness. If the photographer is a surrogate for the filmmaker, as Mulvey suggests, what we see in the opening sequence is the dialectic of control and violence in the act of rendering a subject visible for the cinema, an act which paradoxically is concealed by the apparatus of the cinema / flash itself.

In these examples, formal analysis serves the larger end of argument, not exactly about the film's themes, but about how their language structures their *effects*, or how their choices about formal organization help to convey broader meaning. It bears reiterating that these are not necessarily unconscious effects, although they can be submerged, and neither do they embed some code for which you require a key to unlock the film's secrets; any viewer paying a whit of attention notices the prevalence of extreme close-ups in Carl-Theodor Dreyer's *The Passion of Joan of Arc*; the task becomes to explain how they function, why they matter. (Perhaps they build a point of view that transports the viewer outside of the position of judging Joan as a heretic, as Bordwell's position I cited in Chapter 4 argues; they simulate an alternative to the logic of condemnation and salvation the film proposes as its narrative focus. Or perhaps Dreyer presents, as Bela Balazs argues, "a passionate life-and-death struggle almost exclusively by close-ups of faces," in which "fierce passions, thoughts, emotions, convictions battle" [Balazs 2004: 321]. See with which, if either, you agree.)

If language structures meaning, or if we can find and fix meaning in the cinema, we position ourselves within a hermeneutics of reception, the practice of a quest. If you've ever tried to explain to a friend what the film you just saw was "about," you find yourself stumbling in the realm of meaning-making; if you risk the further effort of condensing into a sound bite what a given film's "message" was, you're in deeper. As you know from both of these experiences, however, the terms fail satisfactorily to translate the experience of watching an interesting film, coming to understand the terms or assumptions of the world it constructs, and bringing those assumptions with you back into the light of day outside the theater or into your everyday world.

"Making meaning" is, of course, a slippery phrase. One constantly thinks, even or especially when one claims to be simply "taken in" by a narrative or an experience. When I watch an abstract film, such as the late Nam June Paik's *Zen for Film* (a film comprised entirely of clear leader, that is, a film entirely without images, in front of which Paik then stands, meditating or performing), I hesitate to attribute a final meaning or message to what I see, but I try energetically, even frantically, to figure out what the filmmaker is asking me to have experienced, to have noticed, to have understood (Renan 1967: 247). When I watch a film urging a more starkly drawn view of the world, such as the anti-Semitic Nazi-era film *Jud Süss* (1940), I understand, with a tremor, that its provocation may have been transparent to those who shared its hateful vision. It may be helpful to shed entirely the idea of a determinate meaning or message, then, in favor of an elaboration of what the film seems to ask us to ponder or to endure. With my students, we frequently formulate this elaboration in terms of a film's *project*.

A film frequently referenced as a model for, commentary upon, and challenge to hermeneutic activity is, of course, *Citizen Kane*. Laura Mulvey opens her short book on *Kane* with Jorge Luis Borges' observation that the film is a "labyrinth without a centre" (Mulvey 1992: 9). Recall how the opening sequence immediately establishes a prohibition (the "no trespassing" sign), transgressed just as quickly by a series of dissolves that transport the camera through the barbed-wire fence on its way to and then into Kane's palace, Xanadu. If the camera functions as a surrogate for the spectator, who then impossibly witnesses Kane uttering his deathbed phrase, "Rosebud," the spectator promptly finds another surrogate in the investigative journalist, Thompson, whose task it becomes to unlock the mystery to this enigmatic dying gasp. Structurally nestled within a series of nonlinear flashbacks, the story of Charles Foster Kane invites questions paralleling those of the spectator's initial predicament, questions precisely about how point of view is linked to meaning, questions about "who knows what?," according to what means of access. The film poses questions, ultimately, about answerability, about views of the world: can one finally attribute a particular meaning to Rosebud, or is the human a mystery that can never be solved?

The structure of *Kane* contributes to our lack of satisfaction in whatever answers we think we encounter. Because Welles presents Thompson's quest in flashback, the viewer meets complicated characters who then recall the life of Kane according to the terms of their proximity: "personal relations, misunderstandings, hopes, love, ambition, disappointment, and so on" (Mulvey 1992: 22). These competing accounts are not only partial and fragmentary, but contradictory. Mulvey also notices how the film offers its own red herrings and false leads, frustrating easy explanations or associative certainty. Reading the sequence following upon Thompson's dispatch to discover the mystery of Rosebud, Mulvey cites the poster (shown only to the film's audience) of Susan Alexander's face accompanied by a bolt of lightning as providing a potential answer (the mystery is answered by Susan). But the sequence piles further puzzles onto this simple explanation:

> The shot [of the poster] sets up a complicity between screen and spectator that is heightened by a sweeping crane shot, the opening shot of Thompson's investigation. Moving down through a skylight, to find Susan in the enclosed space below, the investigative drive of the camera interacts with the *mise-en-scène* to materialise both the space of the film's enigma and the camera's privileged role in the film's subsequent unfolding of its enquiry into the enigma. But the hint at a snap solution to the "Rosebud" enigma is too broad and the juxtaposition too obvious. The spectator instinctively rejects such an easy putting together of two and two and suspects they make five. But the film text has made a gesture to itself as a source of meaning and discovery independent of its protagonists. The responsive spectator senses an invitation to start figuring out the enigma with the camera's collaboration.
>
> (Mulvey 1992: 24)

As with the film's opening sequence, then, the spectator assumes an active, curious, investigative role in relation to the film's characters and the narrative they unfold. If there is no final "meaning" or "message" to the film, it may be that the film is itself about that impossibility.

Other practices of reception emphasize the complexity of meaning-making in different ways. Ideology critique (many examples of which I've cited, if not under this rubric) stitches the project of a film to its socio-cultural location, seeking to understand how films reinforce, challenge, or reveal conceptions of the world that powerfully shape viewers' lives. Another approach derived from phenomenology overthrows the certainty in hermeneutics that the film is in fact an object of the (critic's) subject's scrutiny. Following Merleau-Ponty and others who developed the philosophical arena of phenomenology, film theorists such as Vivian Sobchack (2004) posit a more mobile, transitive, reciprocal understanding of subject–object relations, so that the film itself, understood by most reception studies as an object, instead is seen to interact sensually, carnally, and powerfully with spectators. But the interventions in reception study that represented major interventions in the past quarter-century here have the last word: studies in feminist, critical race, and queer spectatorship and reception. No scholar beginning to work with cinema today can remain untouched by the questions these studies raise.

SPECTATORSHIP AS BRIDGE

If we have bracketed reception studies in this chapter, it is time to return to the holy trinity of production / exhibition / reception to remember how tightly they are bound together and how the division into discrete arenas serves more as an heuristic than as an accurate picture of the beast that is cinema. Genre, as I suggested, serves both as a category of production (whereby individuals or production companies embark upon the self-conscious making of a "romantic comedy" or an "historical epic") and as a description of practices of reception according to generic conventions and expectations. Indeed, production innovations as well as spectatorial habits depend vitally upon the fluidity of this exchange.

This fluidity characterizes the relationship of feminist film theory and practice as well; what I want to suggest in this concluding section is that a cinematic conception largely shaped through feminist reception and analysis translated historically into feminist filmmaking practice not only in the artisanal, experimental, and documentary arenas but also in commercial narrative film. In other words, feminist film criticism began by women in the audience and in the academy noticing how mainstream and dominant film circulated demeaning and narrow stereotypes of women, observations collected in early volumes such as Molly Haskell's 1974 *From Reverence to Rape*. Alongside this form of reception, early scholars began the work of resuscitating buried lives and reputations, making visible the contributions of directors such as the first woman, Alice Guy Blaché, or later directors Ida Lupino or Dorothy Arzner. In the same year (1975), Laura Mulvey wrote an article for the cinema studies magazine *Screen*, "Visual Pleasure and Narrative Cinema," in which she seized the language of psychoanalysis as a weapon to combat the objectification of women under the male gaze produced through the exchange of looks in the cinematic apparatus. Identifying three such looks (that of the spectator at the screen, that of the camera, and that of characters within the film at one another), Mulvey effectively demonstrated how the vision (aesthetic, ideological) of the classical Hollywood cinema is complicit with a menacing patriarchal vision that consigns women to the status of passive objects.

Mulvey, unlike Haskell, made films as well as essays. In those films she sought, alongside other feminist filmmakers, to invent new gazes, new cinematic possibilities for women, and new relationships between men and women onscreen. Other feminist filmmakers in the 1970s such as Akerman (whose *Jeanne Dielman* we encountered previously; see pp. 45–6), Yvonne Rainer, Jane Campion, Joyce Chopra, and others began to tell stories of women's lives previously unrecognized by even the most idiosyncratic and inventive makers of the experimental and underground (largely male) cinema: stories of pregnancy, of fat, of coming of age, of female desire, of women's sensual and sexual pleasures, of housework, of feminist politics, and so on. Shifts in story accompanied shifts in form; Mulvey's own *Riddles of the Sphinx* (1977) is itself an essay in psychoanalytic theory, using fragmented interviews, multiple voices, contested forms of authority, and rich intellectual inquiry to combat the very objectification and fetishization of women's bodies she observed in "Visual Pleasure."

Makers in the 1970s established alternative exhibition circuits and venues (for example women's film festivals and distribution houses such as the still-vibrant Women Make Movies) and alternative critical projects (such as the German journal *Frauen und Film*) to sustain their interventions at the level of form and content. But if *Riddles* isn't screened much these days, or if audiences don't respond immediately to abstract films such as Rainer's *Line* (1970), it's not only because these experiments have yielded to others or have grown dated. To the contrary: feminist theoretical conceptions of the cinema have become axiomatic for contemporary critical practice, so much so that it's virtually impossible to encounter a mention of one of the cinematic gazes – and it's difficult to treat classical cinema without examining their interplay – without a footnote to "Visual Pleasure." Feminist filmmaking practices, too, made enough of an inroad into the commercial mainstream that its gendered grammar is slowly changing, and the line between countercinema and the commercial center is blurring. In *Feminist Hollywood: From 'Born in Flames' to*

'Point Break', film scholar Christina Lane recognizes women not only as images on the screen but as makers in a complex industry and interviews several women, such as Susan Seidelman and Martha Coolidge, who were key to commercial projects in the decades following the initial burst of feminist filmmaking (Lane 2000).

I would hate to be misread here. The picture is not rosy: few women occupy central positions within the Hollywood (or other commercial industrial) hierarchies; the range of women's lives represented on film remains constricted (and, in the U.S. and Europe, largely white). But what requires emphasis is that the dynamic interplay between watching and making that characterized 1970s feminist work remains vital to movements of countercinema. Women filmmakers persist, and the conjoining of makers with distributors and scholars that feminist film inspired also spawned models for countercinemas and counterpublics associated with racial / ethnic visions and with queer cinema. Bristling at the pictures of ourselves on the big screen, makers of color and queer makers respond both critically *and* artistically, creating critiques alongside counterportraits. If the first impulse has been toward arguing for, and making, more "authentic," more "true," more "complex," and more "realistic" representations, recent developments in film theory and practice have proposed new avenues. These, by and large, are the implicit focus of Chapter 6.

BOX 5.3: SUMMARY

Studying film reception frequently involves surveying how actual viewers historically responded or might have responded to films: film reviews, letters to the editor, studio files, theater records, and the like are exciting sources for reception studies of this sort, and you may want to experiment with what they reveal. But reception also describes a broad set of questions about how we, as spectators positioned by the films themselves and by our social roles, respond experientially and intellectually to film. Some activities of reception coincide with the attribution of *value*: top ten lists, prizes at Cannes, thumbs up or down, and cults based around directorial authority. If these tend to assume that audiences respond univocally to relatively transparent film texts, however, other models of reception presume a more active pursuit of engagement or meaning. Several schools of thought expand upon formal analysis to track the very activity of responding to images that attracts us to cinema in the first place. Close analysis can lead to ideological, hermeneutic, phenomeno-logical, and other philosophical formulations of the encounter between spectator and movie. Other routes of response seem to translate more directly into filmmaking: the recent history of feminist and queer projects fuses criticism and creative work into new amalgams, new possibilities.

6

THE FUTURE OF FILM

As cinema begins its second century, many significant questions facing film studies fall into two areas: first, debates about the context in which it might best be studied, as film studies in many arenas morphs and coalesces with visual studies and media studies (not to mention area studies and the study of literature) and with broader developments in the humanities and social sciences (including anthropology, sociology, and psychology); second, questions proliferate in debates about film's specificity and social role as it increasingly takes digital forms and circulates in different ways. This final chapter takes a closing look at the crises of film's identity, beginning in the first section, "Theories of film," with an overview of approaches to film study that determine different positions about film's relation to the digital world and its social role within new configurations of the commodity form and spectatorship. Among these theoretical approaches are Marxism and ideology critique, poststructuralism, psychoanalysis, postmodernism, feminist, queer, and postcolonial. While it is impossible to trace each thoroughly, this section gestures toward the realms of scholarship an advanced student in film studies will engage in by taking up various ways of understanding film's future. The second section, "The future of film," looks toward the future study of film in light of its ongoing death (the deterioration and degradation of film itself) and the birth of new media. Fusing a discussion of the language of new media with a meditation on film as medium, the book ends by urging the reader into the readily accessible universe of DVDs and proliferating digital media to test the premises of film study it has surveyed.

THEORIES OF FILM

PSYCHOANALYSIS

You have encountered theories of film throughout this book, that is, assumptions about what film is, about how best to understand its structure, about how it functions in dialogue with its society. Assumptions about form, assumptions about history, assumptions about social change, assumptions about habits of perception, assumptions about cinema's effects; all of these underpin the previous chapters, and you ought to check them, submit them to scrutiny, as you pursue your own research and viewing. But, as many scholars will tell you, not all thinking about film constitutes a theory of film, that is, a systematic, coherent hypothesis about its working that is argued and tested through evidence. Many conceptions of film theory organize themselves around ideas you have already encountered: the gaze, stardom, authorship, realism, the specificity of film language, the relationship of the image to technology, and so on. Many discussions of cinema now called "theoretical," however, derive from much broader conversations that energize intellectuals from a number of disciplines, including literary studies, philosophy, art history, theater, architecture, and the like. If these formulations of theory present a challenge in the form of a terminological thicket, I urge you to hang in there and not simply to dismiss them as jargon, for I hope to show you how the questions they pose and answer may illuminate aspects of cinema you have not yet considered or encountered in these pages.

Psychoanalysis (what scholar David Bordwell disparages as one of the great intellectual "train-wrecks" of the twentieth century) offered a prime if not *Ur*-example of a theory of how particularly classical narrative cinema functions (Bordwell 2005: Preface). The central presuppositions of psychoanalysis? That children are sexual;

that our childhood sexual lives (fantasies and experiences) shape a part of us, the unconscious, which remains inaccessible but nonetheless structures our later lifeworlds; that the unconscious expresses itself in symptoms but also in dreams and jokes; and that unconscious material has a strong impact upon our adult gendering and sexuality. Briefly, then, psychoanalytic understandings of *film* hypothesize beyond the often-repeated and relatively simple idea that "films are dreams." Films mimic and play with dream logic, of course: Maya Deren's *Meshes of the Afternoon* (1943), or the surrealist experiment by Luis Buñuel and Salvador Dali, *Un Chien Andalou* (1929), invite interpretation as dreams (whatever their makers may have alleged). Psychoanalytic film scholars further propose, however, that film offers, through the characters on screen, representations of "ego-ideals" ("I"s who are larger than life, more beautiful and talented and coordinated and debonair than we will ever be) with whom we – anonymous spectators in a safe, individuating, dark envelope – cannot help but identify and thereby play out the very dramas of gendered and sexual life psychoanalysis posits as foundational to our unconscious formations. In this view, for the spectator the film experience resembles an historical re-enactment, a drama that replays our own stories of entrance into symbolization where we take up, however precariously, our assigned positions within the social order.

Both Freud and Jacques Lacan, the French psychoanalyst whose work influentially guided adaptations of psychoanalysis for film, stress the perilous nature of the pathway to "normal" adult hetero-sexuality as well as the complicated routes pursued by desire itself (Freud 1975 [1905]; Lacan 1998). Following these invigoratingly intricate models of the psyche, film scholars working in the psychoanalytic tradition likewise tend to stress the thwartings, failures, perversions, and ticks revealed through film narrative and the "film text" more generally understood as a form of speech subject to analytic interpretation (much like the speech of the patient or "analysand" on the famous couch seeking the "talking cure"). Among the advances made by psychoanalytic critics, queer film theorist Ellis Hanson enumerates the following:

> They have regarded the "how" of spectatorship as a social and psychological construction. They have sought to develop a theory of subjectivity

that would account for the pleasures of the look and the relationship of those pleasures to gender and sexual identity. They enrich political critiques of cinematic pleasure by theorizing the psychic mechanisms of identification and desire, but they also challenge such critiques by deeming impossible any necessary conjunction, any perfect fit, between ideology and desire, narrative and pleasure, the image and the subject.

(Hanson 1999: 12)

In Chapter 5, following the work of Laura Mulvey, I suggested, perhaps more gently than Bordwell, that the psychoanalytic trail has at the same time led to several impasses, producing nonetheless a robust literature about the dangers and failure of the models it suggests to explain certain forms of visual pleasure, displeasure, engagement, or curiosity regarding the film experience and the film interpreted as text. Through the 1980s and well into the 1990s, in fact, feminist readings in and against psychoanalytic film theory represented one of the most vital and rigorous areas of inquiry in all of the Anglophone humanities. (Revisit the essays in the journals *Screen* and *Camera Obscura* for a taste of what that decade produced.) Not all of them pursued the path Mulvey opened in understanding how Hitchcock and Josef von Sternberg fetishized and punished their female stars; Gaylyn Studlar argued, for example, and to the contrary, that Sternberg's films with Marlene Dietrich developed a masochistic rather than sadistic punishing regime of action and spectatorship (Studlar 1988). Others, including queer scholars, raised questions about the strict gendering of identi- fication, wondering about gay men's devotion to musical icon Judy Garland or lesbian fascination with the phenomenon of cross- dressing in 1930s cinema. A barrage of feminist and queer writing proved that mechanistic "applications" of psychoanalysis to film texts yield little in the way of understanding axes of social life all but ignored by Freud, such as racial difference. Similarly, a reading of Freud and his followers that posited psychoanalysis as an unchanging system led to a sense that its insights tended to be both ahistorical and apolitical. Changes in screening situations and tech- nologies, moreover, raised questions about our immersion in the film text and our unbroken identifications with onscreen surro- gates; identification with the minute figures on our television screens further complicated the model of the overwhelming ego-ideal.

In recent years, however, a number of extremely insightful projects both in psychoanalysis and in film show us that the work of Freud and Lacan (and others such as Jung or Silvan Tompkins, whose work was promoted by literary scholar Eve Kosofsky Sedgwick) remains polyvalent and open to generative understandings. The new translations of Lacan into English by Bruce Fink (whose commentaries guide the reader along wonderful new paths for reading) render previously obdurate passages more pliant, and new writings on affect follow psychoanalytic trails only as faint traces for investigating the material of our speech and the quirks of our murky self-understanding. Film theorists such as D.N. Rodowick and Steven Shaviro demonstrate how central psychoanalytic genealogies are to poststructuralist theory. Finally, the considerable appeal of the "Elvis of cultural theory," the "giant from Lujbljana," Slavoj Žižek, has inspired many scholars to revisit the writings of Lacan through Žižek's readings of popular culture; even if his work tends to use films such as Hitchcock's *Psycho* more as illustrations of his thinking than as critical objects in their own right, his writings exploit popular culture as a sphere of shared reference and as an effective medium through which to convey shared experiences and assumptions about the world.

IDEOLOGY

If psychoanalysis seems recalcitrant on many questions of history, race, and politics, film scholars have continued with other theoretical projects that seem to promise clearer avenues toward unpacking the ways in which film derives its form and material stuff from the world and works in powerful ways upon its spectators. Ideology critique, a strain of Marxist theory, is as central to Žižek's project, for example, as is Lacanian psychoanalysis, and a number of influential film theorists have elaborated a model of ideology that adapts to the configuration of culture, including film, under the pressures of global capitalism. The central presuppositions of ideology critique? The assertion of an inherent relationship between the material conditions of social life, that is to say the economic and social organization of ownership and production, and the historical prevalence or dominance of certain aesthetic forms. The questions then become: How can one describe the *mediation* between political economy and art? How might one read the traces of political economy through film form? How do conceptions of the world (ideology, or what Raymond Williams alternatively called "structures of feeling") take hold in us through film, even or especially when they are not conceptions that correspond to our best interests or, indeed, when they actively work against those interests? How, in other words, do we come to know who we are through artworks that help to structure our own alienation and subjugation?

Ideology critique retains some purchase in a number of domains whose names may or may not be familiar to you: theories of cyberculture, postmodernism, postcoloniality, and areas broadly defined such as cultural studies, media studies, critical race studies (or black cultural studies), feminist and queer studies, studies of border crossings (diaspora, *la frontera*), and so on. The work of British Marxists, in the elaboration of the project that came to be known as cultural studies (itself an unstable moniker), lies at the heart of many of the formulations of the problem of ideology in these various areas, and the questions that animated its early formulations continue to galvanize current work on culture: questions about the social distribution of power and forms of social difference, questions about individual thought and belief and their relation to larger social networks and forces, and questions about the role that mass culture and popular culture (to refer to the distinction discussed in Chapter 5; see p. 104–5) play in sustaining or bringing about change in social formations. If the fields of inquiry listed a moment ago circle around these questions too, they do so while cross-pollinating one another.

We have yet to pursue a satisfactory answer to the central question, however, of how political economy might be understood to produce formal tendencies, or how form might offer an index (not a symptom, not a reference to a deep structure) of political economy. Fredric Jameson's hypothesis, in his much-lauded book *Postmodernism*, is that an artistic style and broader concept called by that name, postmodernism, is the cultural correlate (or, in his terms, the cultural "dominant") of the system of late capitalism:

The fundamental ideological task of the new concept, however, must remain that of coordinating new forms of practice and social and mental habits (this is finally what I take Williams to have had in mind by the notion of a "structure of feeling") with the new forms of economic production and organization thrown up by the modification of capitalism – the new global division of labor – in recent years.

(Jameson 1991: xiv)

"Coordinating" is thus Jameson's synonym here for "mediating," for yoking culture to economy, and he sees that coordination most profoundly in new media forms, such as video and what he calls the "nostalgia film," a category including David Lynch's *Blue Velvet* (1986) alongside Jonathan Demme's film of the same year, *Something Wild*. If the realist novel was the formal correlate of bourgeois vision in the nineteenth century, film and new media, in other words, reveal in their form important shifts in the organization of life under late capitalism, which in turn is thought to be a profoundly global vision: "the vision of a world capitalist system fundamentally distinct from the older imperialism, which was little more than a rivalry between the various colonial powers" (Jameson 1991: xix). Forms of narrative such as the science fiction novel, then, emerge based upon the conditions of possibility of a given era: it becomes fruitful

to stress the conditions of possibility of such a form – and of its emergence and eclipse – less in the existential experience of history of people at this or that historical moment than rather in the very structure of their socioeconomic system, in its relative opacity or transparency, and the access its mechanisms provide to some greater cognitive as well as existential contact with the thing itself.

(Jameson 1991: 284)

Jameson's emphasis on the system itself, in its workings and in its materiality, translates into extremely nuanced and fascinating work on film form. For Matthew Tinkcom, for example, sees "camp," like postmodernism, as a response, and an intellectual one at that, to the baffling effects of modernity; the films of mavericks like Andy Warhol and John Waters, as much as the lavish MGM musicals produced through Arthur Freed's production unit, visualize "the indeterminacies and contradictions of capital and the effects of modernity" through the concealed labors of queer subjects (Tinkcom 2002: 27). Reading those moments at which narrative seems to fail, Tinkcom finds explanations of a film text's formal and aesthetic conception. In this work, theories of cinema nestle within much broader considerations of the movement of capital and the labor that feeds the film industry, while conceptions of "style" or "taste" necessarily expand beyond the specific aesthetic and erotic capacities of cinema. Similarly, taking the global nature of capitalism's reach seriously, Michael Hardt and Antonio Negri propose "Empire" as a concept (not a metaphor) that envelops forms of domination under and resistance to processes of globalization. In these processes (also processes of what they call "postmodernization") cinema encompasses an image of modernity at the same time as it joins in new economies of information and communication that demand new forms of analysis. One can, in other words, read the image of Chaplin as they do for his prophecy of liberation:

> What was really prophetic was the poor, bird-free laugh of Charlie Chaplin when, free from any utopian illusions and above all from any discipline of liberation, he interpreted the "modern times" of poverty, but at the same time linked the name of the poor to that of life, a liberated life and a liberated productivity.
>
> (Hardt and Negri 2000: 159)

At the same time, however, one must situate individual cultural products within the morphing economies of their production, particularly the "massive centralization of control" (Hardt and Negri 2000: 300) characteristic of the quasi-monopolies of transnational infotech and communications corporations. "Empire" struggles to name something different from what postmodernism names, insofar as "Empire" designates the prevalence of new forms of power; in Hardt and Negri's view, both postmodernism (of a lineage less from Jameson than from Lyotard and Baudrillard) and postcolonial critique (of a lineage through Homi Bhabha) are symptoms or effects of – rather than challenges to – the very transition to Empire they seek to describe. Like Jameson, however, they ultimately are interested in massive changes in the globalizing economy and its attendant cultures.

Postmodernism represents, then, one among many attempts to gauge and respond to the mediations between political economy and cultural production. Insofar as they also are attempts to diagnose changes – in the organization and movement of capital, in an epoch's experience of and relation to history, in aesthetic possibilities, in formal constraints – discourses of postmodernism, postcolonialism, and poststructuralism provide robust theoretical frames against which many more local projects within film studies push. If Richard Dyer's conception of stars as social mediators (which I discussed in Chapter 4) holds, for example, how do changes in the post-studio and global (including trans-, inter-, and intranational) era of stars' production shape readings of their new social functions? How, to take the example a step further, do Bollywood stars enable or inhibit discourses of secularism in and beyond India? If the function of authorship shifts in an industry quickly taking advantage of the profits to be reaped from so-called "independent" productions, how might we understand formal innovations in a material light? If (well-off) spectators may now imitate the conditions of theatrical exhibition in their living rooms (with widescreen plasma HDTV [high-definition television] monitors and surround sound), how do previous conceptions of the cinematic apparatus and its role as an ideological machine undergo revision? Questions like these animate much current work in film theory, not uncritically embracing postmodernism or adjacent discourses but instead elaborating the study of cinema within larger social questions.

FEMINIST / QUEER EMBODIMENTS

Another place to witness the efflorescence of film theory in relation to social issues is in the consideration of the body following from feminist interventions in the 1980s through queer work beginning in the 1990s to current work on embodiment through a phenomenological lens. While "the body" pops up in abstracted and dematerialized ways in postmodern theory and in cyberculture (for example in the work of Jean Baudrillard, or even that of Arthur and Marilouise Kroker), those who live in and / or understand the circumstances of embodied difference assert its materiality and its material production through the technologies of the cinema. If feminist theory in its encounter with psychoanalysis alerted us to the objectification of women's bodies onscreen, it also understood that fetishization as a product of fear, thereby noting the immense power of the cinema in the reproduction of psychic and social roles. Masculinity and femininity seemed, on the one hand, to be so rigidly codified through commercial narrative film that the cinema ought largely to be treated as an engine of oppression, churning out stereotypes and strengthening imbalances in power between men and women by rendering women mostly passive eroticized objects for active male protagonists who propel the narrative forward. On the other hand, the opposite seemed equally true: subject any given film to a rigorous enough reading and you'll see immediately how leaky and unstable these roles are; that masculinity accrues to women and femininity to men, that bodies have complicated relationships to power and authority, that eroticism is by no means contained in (human) bodies, that spectatorial bodies are no mere "positions" but lived embodiments, sighing, fidgety, excitable (or bored). The first feminist studies of pornography, such as Linda Williams' *Hardcore*, complicated the analysis even further, since pornography demands a different intersubjective relationship (a polite way of saying a relationship of direct stimulation) between text and spectator. Identification, activity, gender, and pleasure refuse to line up neatly, in other words, with feminist political assessments, rendering the question of how to engage cinematic embodiment in need of illumination from other sources.

Queer film practices and theory help in thinking through the politics of embodiment, for many of the most important queer films of the past decades emerge from AIDS activism and the immensely vexed and contradictory issues of representation surrounding the body of the person with AIDS (PWA). Mainstream media, including documentary and narrative films, subjected the PWA to a pathologizing and even criminalizing gaze, cleaving the world into binaries such as the healthy and the infected, the normal and the perverse, the innocent and the guilty, the West and the rest, the clean and the tainted, and so forth. Summoning the media's voices of authority through devices such as documentary talking heads or the manipulation of identification and empathy in the narrative film, homophobic and hostile media industries painted sympathetic portraits only sporadically and usually by cordoning off a sphere of the innocent, the white, the straight, and the clean from other PWAs thought in some manner to "deserve it."

Media activists and artists countered, but the production of self-portraits raised vital questions about the mediations that are always endemic to representation. That is, to present a more realistic, more political, more inclusive, more powerful or more enabling picture of AIDS is to make hard choices with the same tools. How does one represent the reality of death? Through what genre: the social documentary, the love story, the musical? What is more real, individual suffering or collective triumph? Who adjudicates the line between "representative" and "specific"? What forms are adequate to articulate shared trauma? What, to use Douglas Crimp's terms, are the historical and particular relationships between mourning and militancy, between grief and social action (Crimp 2002)? Load these questions onto weak, sick bodies facing so-called "premature" death, bodies marked with opportunistic infections such as the purple lesions of Karposi's sarcoma (KS), pneumonia, or decaying eyesight due to cytomegalovirus (CMV); and then factor in the angry, transformative, world-changing collective spirit of AIDS activism, with the talents of those armies of queer laborers in the entertainment industries from graphic designers to musicians to, of course, filmmakers. What results, in that body of work we refer to as AIDS film (from the 1980s to the present, from Los Angeles to Cape Town), helps us to see how bodies are always framed (Hallas forthcoming), never contained easily in the envelope of the individual human, and always therefore requiring careful and detailed attention, even loving description. Bodies in AIDS cinema flow on and offscreen as witnesses and as lovers, as disintegrating and diminished or as ghosts and angels, as microscopic cells and as morphing viruses, as surfaces and skins and as holes and caverns.

Giving the abstracted "body" some actual flesh, some life as an embodied specific body, is the task, finally, of theoretical work that carries the torch of feminist and queer engagements with body politics. Vivian Sobchack's most recent book, *Carnal Thoughts* (2004), for example, combines autobiography and anecdote with existential phenomenology based upon the philosophy of Maurice Merleau-Ponty. Schematically, the latter stresses the imbrication of subject and object, subjectivity and objectivity, in lived experiences: "existential phenomenology is a philosophically [sic] grounded on the carnal, fleshy, objective foundations of subjective consciousness as it engages and is transformed by and in the world" (Sobchack 2004: 2). It provides an avenue for engagement and reflection that is, in other words, materialist and directed toward both aesthetics and ethics. For Sobchack, cinema serves as an archive of a shared, common, or general understanding of embodied experiences, similar to the resonant common sense embedded in ordinary language; it also serves to provide dense meditations in its own right on embodiment. Bringing to cinema her own embodied experiences as a woman, a middle-aged woman, and an amputee (after a series of many cancer surgeries), Sobchack weaves an intersubjective and, I suppose, interobjective account of embodied experience to and of the cinema (from David Cronenberg's adaptation of *Crash* [1997] to the metaphysics of the films of Krzysztof Kieslowski). As with exciting work on affect (in a lineage drawing from Deleuze), Sobchack's investigation of embodiment keeps alive tensions between specificity and theoretical reflection, between text and response, between the ordinary and the extraordinary in forging a new avenue for film theory.

REALISM

Finally, in this short survey of lively strands of film theory, much current work is in conversation with earlier debates about realism (represented paradigmatically by Bazin in Chapter 1's closing sections). Recall that early film theory divided between theories valorizing realism and theories valorizing artifice: realism versus what came to be called formalism. On the realist end of the spectrum, Bazin and others such as Siegfried Kracauer and Stanley Cavell understood film to be tied, as photography is, materially to its referent. In Bazin's terms, film was "objective" insofar as an actual strip of film carried with it the trace of the referent or object it recorded. A film made of a profilmic chair, in other words, carried the objective imprint of that chair. Using terms drawn from linguistics, film bears an indexical relationship to its referent; there is a causal relationship between the filmic image and the referent it records. Bazin, as you now know, extended this referential nature of film to a stylistic set of preferences that allowed for contemplation of film's "objective" nature (the long shot, composition in depth, and so on). On the formalist end of the spectrum, Sergei Eisenstein and his Soviet compatriot Dziga Vertov praised film's ability to produce its own realities, to create, to reorganize, to reshape what is into what might be. A chair could become a throne or a chariot, or it could develop a life of its own as a theater chair, through the manipulation of images, particularly through montage, into new forms and possibilities.

If the realism vs. formalism opposition never was completely codified or stark, it also became subsumed by developments in film theory that alleged realism to have been, "always already" as the phrase has it, a construction. Realism, that is, is as much effect as cause, as much a product of conventional situations and assumptions as a ground toward which cinema might move. Renewed interest in realism is due, then, to the ways in which hypotheses of constructivism hold purchase in a number of different critical discussions, from gender and queer studies (in the work of Judith Butler, for example, who examines Jennie Livingston's film on drag balls, *Paris is Burning*, through its discourses of performance) to poststructuralist theory (Deleuze) and theories of history.

Debates about realism also drove a number of projects grouped under the heading of Third Cinema, a misleading singular name for diverse films about anti-colonial and anti-imperial struggles for national liberation, from Africa to Cuba. On the one hand, as you might anticipate, these films confronted the question of how to represent struggles of the people who had no means for such representation under the oppression of their colonizers or who inherited, post-independence, the representational regimes (grammars, habits, institutions) of those very oppressors. (Three very different examples illuminate these conundrums: Ousmane Sembene's 1966 *La Noire de . . . / Black Girl*, Gillo Pontecorvo's 1966 *Battle of Algiers*, and Tomás Guttiérez Alea's 1959 *Memories of Underdevelopment*.) On the other hand, these films needed literally to invent new realities, new nations emerging in the process of decolonization, which included the decolonization of the mind as well as of the image. What forms could best convey or contain the tensions between tradition and the new, between the individual and the collective, between the psychic and the social, between the family and the nation, and so on?

There are no answers, really, to the question (just as there are no helpful answers to Bazin's question "What is cinema?"). The displacement of the rubric of Third Cinema by other terms and movements (postcolonial to black British to AIDS cinema) demonstrates, however, that realism has always embedded political questions, questions about the vision of the world that cinema can produce and inspire. Questions of realism paradoxically persist the more that the technologies of the film image fuse with other (new and old) technologies of image-making and reproduction, such as video, installation art, and, of course, the world of the digital. In what follows, I pose questions about film's future in terms of the past you know it to harbor.

THE FUTURE OF FILM

If this plurality of approaches to film alerts us to a thriving and exciting inquiry that persists under the auspices of film studies, it is also true that a number of other disciplines now encompass, speak to, or otherwise engage film studies. Media studies, digital media, digital art, art history, visual studies, visual culture, cultural studies, media convergence, new media; these are some of their names. And these are some of their objects: cyberdemocracy, 'net art, online cultures, cyberspace, blogs, podcasting, online identity and the virtual body, interactivity, the digital image, digital cinema, collective intelligence, ideas of interface and interactivity, simulation, computer culture. There are undoubtedly others, and much of the point of the changing landscape is to emphasize the "new" in "new media," the emergent, difficult to detect, uneven, diffuse, dispersed, even contradictory effects and manifestations thereof. These "new" forms feed upon, without displacing, radio, broadcast television, cable, satellite, video, theatrical exhibition, print journalism, and, of course, cinema.

Despite the frequent emphasis on the new, however, it is equally possible to place an emphasis on the continuity of new media with previous forms, such as the cinema, as to mark divergences. Lev Manovich, in his especially interesting book *The Language of New Media* (2001), tries to build a "bottom up" (as opposed to speculative or *a priori*) approach to new media by specifying its constituent principles, all of which are to be found in the convergence of the computer and the cinema: numerical presentation, modularity, automation, variability, and transcoding. In his view, the tour that cinema takes in the twentieth century toward realism and indexical representation is a path among others, insofar as it largely left behind the construction of alternative worlds through hand-painting, say, or other ways of animating images. Today, in its digital form, cinema might be seen to be returning to these practices at its origin, such that digital compositing (of which I spoke in Chapter 2) is understood as another kind of animation: "Consequently, cinema can no longer be clearly distinguished from animation. It is no longer an indexical media technology but, rather, a subgenre of painting" (Manovich 2001: 295).

What, then, of realism? In Manovich's view, as in Bazin's, as I suggested, the real is approached only asymptotically, never achieved. Manovich stresses the additive nature of what we might call the realism-effect, whereby successively new technologies reveal the faults of previous claims to realism:

> Each new technological development (sound, panchromatic stock, color) points out to viewers just how "unrealistic" the previous image was and also reminds them that the present image, even though more realistic, will also be superseded in the future – thus constantly sustaining the state of disavowal.
>
> (Manovich 2001: 186)

Digital cinema thus continues a project begun long ago, further developing a form that is the product of certain variables and potentialities, just as some of its cherished forms (such as narrative) yield to others (such as the database).

Manovich's emphasis on the continuity of digital cinema with cinema's previous incarnations provides a helpful antidote against hand-wringing Puritanism that worries about medium specificity. From a similar perspective, although in much more concrete terms, scholar Stephen Prince evaluates processes of digital manipulation in terms of their effects on cinematic representation and viewer response; he suggests that the digitally or computer-designed image (CGI) challenges ideas of realism that are based solely upon conceptions of photography (indexicality) and instead proposes a form of "perceptual realism," "the kinds of linkages that connect the represented fictionalized reality of a given film to the visual and social coordinates of our own three-dimensional world" (Prince 1996: 27, 33).

Yet these observations only begin to open onto questions about how new media will *function*: does the new media landscape offer greater opportunities for public participation? For coalition building? For innovative art? For research and teaching? For fresh thinking? Who will own the new media? Who will control it? These questions animate, as it were, current discussions in the public sphere, and they should, since it is not simply a matter of building theory that can accommodate new media but building worlds that benefit from it, too. In the few remaining pages of this book, I survey the context for this new landscape, along with a few models of engaging new media that I find empowering and exciting, in the hopes that you will update and expand the list.

If film, then, belongs to this new media landscape, it does so as a dimension of culture, and culture itself is changing. As George Yúdice argues, in a useful polemic against the tendency to over-attribute "agency" to cultural producers, the new media landscape is characterized by transnational administration and investment (governed by Western law) and by the commodification of local difference. Within the dominant frame of neoliberalism – assaults on labor, privatization, the elimination of state programs such as welfare, trade liberalization, and the lowering of wages – grassroots movements and international non-governmental organizations turn their focus away from state power to culture, "a resource already targeted for exploitation by capital (e.g., in the media, consumerism, and tourism) and a foundation for resistance against the ravages of that very same economic system" (Yúdice 2003: 6).

Privatization shrinks the public sphere and exacerbates the effects of the digital divide (in which the West and the wealthy have access to digital technologies while the rest and the poor remain unconnected). A new international division of cultural labor emerges. In the face of this imploding and volatile public sphere (where museums, film festivals, digital showcases, and the like face daily threats of de-funding), cinema needs fresh voices beyond those we currently dub the "independent" sphere (a form of outsourcing or flexible specialization resulting in largely white,

English-language films that provide little in the way of counter-discourses or counter-images to the commercial narrative cinema). Furthermore, authorship in the film industry resides, as Yúdice notes, increasingly in the hands of producers and distributors rather than filmmakers, "such that 'creators' are now little more than 'content providers'" (Yúdice 2003: 18). Where ought we to turn to find those fresh voices, those who will produce counter-discourses and new images?

Patricia Zimmermann finds them in those practices disenfranchised by transnational media corporations: radical political documentaries, experimental forms. In her book *States of Emergency* her aim is

> to restore public space to independent documentary practices positioned outside of the spheres of commercial exchange relations. These works operate within other, more oppositional networks of production, distribution, exhibition, circulation, and political struggle, necessary outposts that reject the silencing of discourse and dissent. Social, historical, and political contexts are inscribed and enfolded into these works. The documentaries cannot be categorized exclusively by genre, formal strategies, identity, modes of address, or content.
>
> (Zimmermann 2000: xx)

Like Yúdice, Zimmermann refuses easy optimism. In the works she excavates, she finds (and makes) unexpected alliances and uneasy contradictions.

The films of a collective known as Big Noise are a good example. On their website (where you can buy and stream their works) they define themselves: "Big Noise is a not-for-profit, all-volunteer collective of media-makers around the world, dedicated to circulating beautiful, passionate, revolutionary images" (www.bignoisefilms. com). Among those images are films (*Zapatista, Black and Gold, This Is What Democracy Looks Like, The Fourth World War*) and what they describe as "tactical media," such as a short film made in collaboration with Paper Tiger Television on immediate responses in New York City to the 9/11 attacks, showing the development of a nascent peace movement in solidarity with other movements for economic and social justice, or *Storm from the Mountain*, a short piece that follows the Zapatista caravan through twelve Mexican states.

Big Noise would not be possible without the web, which it uses to send images from cinematographer to editor, from Mexico or Iraq to New York or elsewhere, and to stream its films to a world-wide audience. Updating the projects of radical documentarians to the twenty-first century, Big Noise adopts popular forms rather than scorns them: their musical contributors include Manu Chao, Asian Dub Foundation, Múm, Moosaka, Cypher AD, and DJ C for *The Fourth World War*, while *This Is What Democracy Looks Like* features music by Rage Against the Machine, DJ Shadow, and Anne Feeney (and narration by Susan Sarandon and Michael Franti). Hip and passionate, their films also pose problems for their intended audiences; my students have found them driven by simplified logics and forms, dependent upon heroizing and idealizing strategies. At the same time, the films function often less as reportage or as arguments than as witnesses: they document, for example, the very violence against anti-globalization protests that they present as evidence of repression, and that video footage might then be used as evidence against police violence.

Other forms of witness are important to new documentaries, whether in Ursula Biemann's clandestine footage of a ride to a *maquiladora* – in her video essay on the Mexican–U.S. border town of Ciudad Juarez, where U.S. multinational corporations assemble electronic and digital equipment just across from El Paso, Texas – called *Performing the Border* (1999) – or in the testimonies of mothers of the Plaza de Mayo in Argentina in *Las Madres: The Mothers of Plaze de Mayo* (Susana Muñoz and Lourdes Portillo, 1985). Documenting the traumas of AIDS, makers refused to be silent in the face of devastating loss and generated powerful new graphic styles and elegiac forms in the process. Tom Joslin and Mark Massi's film *Silverlake Lake: The View from Here* performs the almost unimaginable act of documenting the director's own death, in that filmmaker Tom Joslin begins to record the ravages of AIDS when he and his lover, Mark Massi, are diagnosed with the "full-blown" version of the disease, only to die in the process (Joslin's friend and colleague Peter Friedman then edited the footage for the final film). Inspired by AIDS activism and its graphic sophistication, the artists collective THINK AGAIN! usurps public space in guerilla fashion, by wheat-pasting, stickering, and otherwise covering public surfaces with radical artworks; an

"Income Gap: An American Classic" sticker (mimicking the clothing chain's logo) next to an ATM (or in the UK, cash machine) read, "In 1998, the U.S. revoked the rights of immigrants, revoked welfare, and kicked one million children into poverty. In the same year, the wealthiest 10% of Americans owned over 70% of the nation's wealth." THINK AGAIN! uses the internet to disseminate its work (through its website www.agitart.org), but it also mines the visual strategies of new media for its forms of critique. Aware that the nexus of technology and representation is central to new mediascapes, critical artists intervene by expanding and complicating the ground of political intervention.

Examples, of course, could be multiplied, from the pirated critique of alien movies in Alex Rivera's *Día de la Indepencia* (1997) to DeeDee Halleck's *Gringo in Mañanaland* (1995), an assemblage of more than 700 clips from Hollywood films, educational films, industrial films, and newsreels that re-narrates U.S.–Latin American relations as a story of cultural imperialism. The larger point to draw from these examples, however, is that new media propose new forms of engagement, critique, and analysis. If the future of film is in peril, insofar as makers trade Bolex 16mm cameras for Sony digital video ones, so be it, but the study of images and the world of arguments, fantasies, and possibilities they contain will live in your good hands.

BOX 6.1: SUMMARY

The changing nature of college and university curricula and disciplinary divisions lands film study in a number of different locations: you may be a student in an English department, a communications school, an art division, or a cultural studies classroom. Film studies as a discourse thus finds itself in conversation with a number of broader critical endeavors, and theories of film converse with them as well. Psychoanalysis, ideology critique and cultural studies, postmodernism, feminism, queer theory: all of these projects extend across the humanities and help us to think about the future of studying film in the context of a changing world. Likewise, new forms of cinema force us to clarify what film studies will have meant at the dawn of the new century. If we retain a sense of engagement and fascination with the image, combined with a curiosity about film's role in inspiring new forms of social life, we will have bequeathed something durable and vital to you, the next generation of film scholars.

GLOSSARY

180° rule belonging to the system of **continuity editing**, the rule that establishes the axis of action, a line running perpendicular to the camera, such that the camera is understood to have to stay on the same side of this line for each of the subsequent **shots**, preserving **screen direction**.

30° rule belonging to the system of **continuity editing**, the rule that one should vary **camera angle** shot to **shot** by at least 30° (to avoid **jump cuts**).

aperture an adjustable opening in the camera that controls the amount of light admitted.

axis of action *see* **180° rule**.

backlighting placing a light behind the subject to be filmed.

best boy originating from the description of the crew member most appropriate for promotion to supervisor; the chief assistant of the **gaffer** or **key grip**.

blockbuster a term both of film **production** and of **reception**, a film with enormous financial success, mass appeal, global circulation.

booms a long pole used to suspend microphones to record sound.

camera angle the angle of the camera in relation to that which it records.

camera distance the distance between the camera and that which it records, measured in anthropomorphic scale, described by extreme long **shot**, long shot, medium long shot or plan americain, medium shot, medium close-up, close-up, and extreme close-up.

camera movement the movement of the camera during a single **shot**, including tilting, **panning**, **tracking**, and so on.

canted frame the use of a **camera angle** that departs from the horizontal or vertical planes.

casting the practice and business of hiring actors to play characters and roles in a movie.

chiaroscuro extreme **lighting** contrast emphasizing blacks and whites.

cinematography the term of formal analysis that encompasses everything to do with the camera.

classical Hollywood cinema a style of filmmaking involving a cohesive and linear (cause and effect) **narrative** structure, **continuity editing**, the use of *mise-en-scène* that perpetuates "cinematic *realism*," cultural stereotypes or expectation of social plausibility, **genre** plausibility, principal causal agent is a character with clear-cut goals and problems.

continuity editing a system developed through the **classical Hollywood** system to ensure coherence of space and time.

conventions habits of film grammar or **genre** that are repeated and expected.

costume one of six elements of *mise-en-scène*.

craning camera movement above or below the plane of action achieved by placing the camera on a crane.

cross-cutting a form of **editing** that indicates simultaneity, cutting between one place of action and another.

cut a form of **editing** that simply joins two **shots** together.

dailies *see* **rushes**.

deep focus a combination of deep space, which is a set (an element of *mise-en-scène*) that allows for action on many planes, and camera **aperture** and focus (elements of **cinematography**) that keeps many planes in sharp focus, called depth of field.

deep space *see* **deep focus**.

depth of field *see* **deep focus**.

diegetic all those sounds and images which belong to the implied world of the film in a **narrative** film.

dissolve a form of **editing** that joins two **shots** together such that the first remains visible for a period of time while the second appears, creating temporary **superimposition** of the two. Dissolves vary in length.

distribution the business and avenues of a film's movement from **production** to **exhibition**, including publicity and promotion.

dolly a wheeled cart built to accommodate a movie camera.

dollying a form of **camera movement** on the ground in which the camera **travels** on a **dolly**.

Dutch angles *see* **canted frame**.

editing, edits ways of joining lengths of film or different **shots** together, including the **cut**, the **dissolve**, the **fade**, the **wipe**, and the **iris**.

emulsion the light-sensitive chemical coating on the **film stock** that determines the film's speed (measurement of light sensitivity).

exhibition initially, the projection of motion pictures on theatre screens; now encompasses the business of exhibiting films on multiple sites.

exposure the length of time at **aperture** setting at which film in the camera is exposed to light.

eye light a light set directed at a figure's eye to produce sparkling.

eyeline match a form of **editing**, in the system of **continuity editing**, joining a first **shot** of a character looking **offscreen** to that which he or she is meant to see in a second shot.

fade-in / fade-out a type of edit in which an image fades to black (or a blank screen) or the opposite, in which black fades to an image.

figure behavior the term formal analysis reserves for anything figures (actors, animals) do within a given **shot** (movement, acting, speaking, etc.).

fill light a secondary light source in the **three-point lighting** system, used primarily to "fill" in shadows.

film noir a film movement in the United States from the 1940s through the 1960s that emphasized the dark, seedy, gritty elements of urban life, usually refracted through the fatal experiences of men; also has come to designate a style of film characterized by **low-key** lighting, male characters associated with the underworld and the femmes fatales whom they pursue.

film stock the actual unprocessed film covered with light-sensitive **emulsion** that passes through the camera.

flashback / flashforward within the system of **continuity editing**, a form of temporal manipulation where a previous event is inserted within the film's present (or where a future event is there inserted).

focal length of a camera's **lens**, the distance between the film plane and the focal point (optical center of the lens) when the lens is focused at infinity, measured in millimeters, and differentiating between prime lenses of a fixed focal length and zoom lenses of variable focal length.

Foley artist named after early practitioner Jack Foley, the artist responsible for recreating incidental sound effects (such as footsteps) in synchronization with the image.

found footage *see* **stock**.

fps (frames per second) *see* **frame**.

frame, framing the segment of film exposed by the camera and subsequently by the projector. Sound film runs through the camera and projector at a rate of 24 fps (frames per second). Framing involves isolating that which the camera will record.

gaffer the head of the electrical department, who is responsible for the design and implementation of a film's **lighting** plan.

gauge the width of the **film stock**, measured in millimeters.

genre a category of both **production** and **reception** referring to film type (western, comedy, thriller, horror, documentary, and so on).

glamor property of stars achieved through labor (of **make-up** artists, **hair** stylists, **costume** designers, etc.) that is naturalized as belonging to the star him- or herself.

graphic match a principle of **continuity editing** whereby two **shots** are joined together on the basis of their graphic similarities.

hair (styling) one of six elements of *mise-en-scène*.

high-key a style of **lighting**, using the **three-point lighting** system, which produces relatively even light with few shadows.

historicism a school of criticism devoted to recreating the historical context out of which an artwork emerged.

implied space *see* **offscreen space**.

iris a type of edit in which the image opens or closes as an **aperture** does to or from black.

jump cut the effect of violating the **30° rule**, in which figures appear to jump in the **frame** as the result of **cuts**.

key grip the chief of a group of grips, responsible for moving lights, **dolly** tracks, cranes, and scenery.

key light the main light source in the **three-point lighting** system.

kicker in a **three-point lighting** system, a directional light from the back, off to one side of the subject, usually from low angle opposite the **key light**, that helps to separate the figure from the background.

Kuleshov effect the thesis, derived from Lev Kuleshov's experiments, that in the broad sense spectators will create unity from juxtaposed images, and the more narrow sense that, in the absence of an establishing **shot**, spectators will create spatio-temporal continuity between two juxtaposed shots.

lens round glass with two refracting surfaces for the camera, varying in quality and **focal length**.

lighting one of six elements of *mise-en-scène*.

line producer the producer responsible for managing every issue and aspect of making a particular film (unlike an executive producer or associate producer, a line producer works on one film at a time).

location an element of **setting**.

low-key a style of **lighting**, using the **three-point lighting** system, which produces high contrast and strong shadows.

magazine an attachment to the camera that holds film.

make-up one of six elements of *mise-en-scène*.

Marxism a school of thought that emphasizes the relationship of culture to a society's **mode** and relations of **production**, i.e. private ownership of the film industry under capitalism, and the role of culture in class and other social antagonisms.

match on action a principle of **editing** whereby two **shots** are joined together to follow a character's action from one to the next.

matte shot a form of **process shot** or composite in which different areas of the image are photographed separately and combined through laboratory work.

mise-en-scène comprising setting / props, lighting, costume, hair, make-up, and **figure behavior**.

mode of production *see* **Marxism**.

montage Sergei Eisenstein's term for a system of composition of elements within **shots** and juxtaposing shots in order to produce response and new meaning. Also the French word for **editing**.

montage sequence a form of **editing** that compresses time radically and shows the passage of time through brief **shots** joined together.

motif a repeated element of *mise-en-scène*, **editing**, sound, or **cinematography**..

narrative a chain of events in a cause–effect relationship.

negative a type of film from which positive prints are struck.

non-diegetic those sounds and images that are not assumed to belong to the diegesis, i.e. credit sequences, musical **scores** meant for the ears of the spectator alone, and so on.

offscreen space the space implied in the six directions of space **framed** in a given **shot** (to the left, right, above, below, in front, behind).

panning a form of **camera movement** in which the camera remains stationary on a horizontal axis but moves on its vertical axis.

parallel editing *see* **cross-cutting**.

persistence of vision the physiological / psychological phenomenon whereby spectators retain an image on the eye's retina for a brief period after the eye is exposed to that image, which together with the **Kuleshov effect** explains how we perceive coherent cinematic motion from a **sequence** of still images.

plot all that spectators see and hear (as opposed to the story, which is all that is implied but not given by the plot).

principal photography the filming of the major scenes of a given film involving the lead actors.

print *see* **negative**.

process shot a type of **shot** created in the laboratory by combining elements from several different shots into one (such as a **matte**).

production all aspects of film-making including the stages of pre-production, production, and post-production.

production design the process of conceiving of the overall look of the movie.

profilmic that which appears before the camera to be filmed.

props one of six elements of *mise-en-scène*.

racking / racked focus changing focus within a **shot**.

real time equivalence between an action's duration and its **screen duration**.

rear projection a form of **process shot** where an image is projected behind the action, all of which is then filmed.

reception as distinct from **exhibition**, the responses of spectators to particular films.

release date the date on which a film is planned to be released from **distribution** into **exhibition** in theaters.

reverse shot *see* **shot–reverse shot**.

rushes also known as dailies, the first positive prints made from the **negatives** filmed on the previous day (viewed by the director to track actors' performances and the progress of **principal photography**).

score music played or composed for the film's soundtrack.

screen direction the direction of movement onscreen, i.e. from screen right to screen left.

screen duration the length of time an event or action is onscreen.

screenplay a script written to be produced as a movie.

script supervisor formerly known as a script girl, the person who is responsible for tracking which scenes have been filmed, the extent to which what has been filmed differs from the script, and therefore for tracking continuity (creating a lined script).

sequence a series of **shots** joined together by **editing** and united in time and space.

setting, set one of six elements of *mise-en-scène*.

shot an exposed and unedited length of film.

shot duration a measurement of **shot** length.

shot–reverse shot a pattern of **editing**, usually of conversations, in which a two-shot (**shot** of two people) is followed by a shot of one person taken from an angle over the shoulder of the other and then a shot of the second person from a similar perspective. Used to secure the idea of both being present in the same time and space.

shutter on a camera and projector that element that opens and closes to emit light.

sound stage a large indoor area for filming in which all aspects of sound and light can be controlled.

stardom the social institution of film stars, including stars themselves, their personae, discourses about stardom, the apparatuses of film promotion and publicity, and so on.

stock type of film varying by **gauge**, speed, black and white or color, reversal or **negative**, but also, as in "stock footage" or "found footage," film shot by one maker and used by another.

story *see* **plot**.

storyboard a series of drawings of every planned **shot** for a given film.

story time the implied length of time over which the story takes place.

studio corporate form of industrial film organization in which all types of film **production** personnel work under contract to a single studio.

superimposition simultaneous presence of two different **shots** onscreen, as in a **dissolve**.

take *see* **shot**.

temporal ellipses gaps of time implied within a **narrative** film.

three-point lighting combination of **key**, **back**, and **fill lights**.

tie-ins commodities / products associated with films (or placed within them) that are marketed to spectators.

tilting form of **camera movement** in which the camera remains stationary on its vertical axis but rotates on its horizontal one.

tinting method of coloring images on a single **negative** (as opposed to three-color processes involving multiple negatives).

tracking form of **camera movement** in which the camera travels on the ground on a track or on a truck.

traveling *see* **tracking**.

treatment a roughly ten-page abridged script, usually summarizing the major scenes and central characters of a proposed movie.

trucking *see* **tracking**.

typage system of **casting** according to social conventions and expectations.

voice-over a sound technique in which a person usually not present onscreen provides narration or reflection.

wipe form of edit in which one **shot** replaces another by pushing it across or down the screen.

BIBLIOGRAPHY

Adorno, Theodor (1994) *The Stars Down to Earth and Other Essays on the Irrational in Culture*, edited with an introduction by Stephen Crook, London: Routledge.

Allen, Robert (1996) "Manhattan Myopia; or, Oh! Iowa!," *Cinema Journal* 35(3).

Anger, Kenneth (1975) *Hollywood Babylon*, San Franciso, CA: Straight Arrow Books.

Balazs, Bela (1985) "Theory of the Film: Sound," in Elisabeth Weis and John Belton (eds) *Film Sound: Theory and Practice*, New York: Columbia University Press.

—— (2004) "The Face of Man," in Leo Braudy and Marshall Cohen (eds.) *Film Theory and Criticism*, 6th edition, Oxford: Oxford University Press; first published in 1945.

Bazin, André (1997) *Bazin at Work: Major Essays and Reviews from the Forties and Fifties*, translated from the French by Alain Piette and Bert Cardullo, edited by Bert Cardullo, New York and London: Routledge.

Bellafante, Gina (1999) "Designing Woman," *Time* (February 22) 153(7): 82.

Bellour, Raymond (2000) "System of a Fragment (on *The Birds*)," *The Analysis of Film*, ed. Constance Penley, Bloomington, IN: Indiana University Press.

Bogue, Ronald (2003) *Deleuze on Cinema*, London: Routledge.

Bordwell, David (1981) *The Films of Carl-Theodor Dreyer*, Berkeley, CA: University of California Press.

—— (2000) *Planet Hong Kong: Popular Cinema and the Art of Entertainment*, Cambridge, MA: Harvard University Press.

—— (2005) *The Cinema of Eisenstein*, with a new preface by the author, London: Routledge.

Bordwell, David and Thompson, Kristin (1993) *Film Art: An Introduction*, New York: McGraw-Hill, Inc.; first published in 1979.

Bordwell, David, Staiger, Janet and Thompson, Kristin (1985) *The Classical Hollywood Cinema: Film Style and Mode of Production to 1960*, New York: Columbia University Press.

Braudy, Leo and Cohen, Marshall (2004) *Film Theory and Criticism*, 6th edition, Oxford: Oxford University Press; first published in 1974.

Buscombe, Edward (ed.) (1988) *The BFI Companion to the Western*, New York: Atheneum.

Cherchi Usai, Paolo (2001) *The Death of Cinema: History, Cultural Memory and the Digital Dark Age*, London: BFI Publishing.

Cohan, Steven and Hark, Ina Rae (eds.) (1997) *The Road Movie Book*, London: Routledge.

Cook, David (2004) *A History of Narrative Film*, New York and London: W.W. Norton and Company; first published in 1981.

Corrigan, Timothy and White, Patricia (2004) *The Film Experience: An Introduction*, New York and Boston, MA: Bedford-St. Martin's.

Crimp, Douglas (2002) *Melancholia and Moralism: Essays on AIDS and Queer Politics*, Cambridge, MA: MIT Press.

Crowe, Cameron (2000) *Almost Famous*, London: Faber and Faber.

Crust, Kevin (2005) "Gruesome Trip into the Outback," *Los Angeles Times* (Friday December 22).

Deleuze, Gilles (1986) *Cinema 1: The Movement-Image*, Minneapolis, MN: University of Minnesota Press; first published in 1983.

—— (1989) *Cinema 2: The Time Image*, Minneapolis, MN: University of Minnesota Press; first published in 1985.

Dickson, W.K.L. and Dickson, Antonia (2000) *History of the Kinetograph, Kinetoscope, and Kinetophonograph*, New York: Museum of Modern Art; first published in 1895.

Dixon, Wheeler Winston (2005) *Lost in the Fifties: Recovering Phantom Hollywood*, Carbondale, IL: Southern Illinois University Press.

Dunne, John Gregory (1997) *Monster*, New York: Vintage Books.

Dyer, Richard (1980) *Stars*, London: BFI Publishing.

—— (ed.) (1984) *Gays and Film*, New York: Zoetrope.

—— (2002) *The Culture of Queers*, London: Routledge.

Egoyan, Atom and Balfour, Ian (2004) *Subtitles: On the Foreignness of Film*, Cambridge, MA: Massachusetts Institute of Technology and Alphabet City Media, Inc.

Feuer, Jane (1982) *The Hollywood Musical*, London: BFI Publishing.

Fish, Stanley (1980) *Is There a Text in this Class? The Authority of Interpretive Communities*, Cambridge, MA: Harvard University Press.

Forgacs, David (2000) *Rome, Open City*, London: BFI Publishing.

Freud, Sigmund (1975) *Three Essays on the Theory of Sexuality*, with an introductory essay by Steven Marcus, translated and newly edited by James Strachey, New York: Basic Books; first published in 1905.

Gunning, Tom (1990) "The Cinema of Attractions," in T. Elsaesser and A. Barker (eds.) *Early Cinema: Space, Frame, Narrative*, London: BFI Publishing.

Hallas (forthcoming) *Reframing Bodies: AIDS, Bearing Winess, and the Queer Moving Image*, Durham, NC: Duke University Press.

Hanson, Ellis (ed.) (1999) *Out Takes: Essays on Queer Theory and Film*, Durham, NC: Duke University Press.

Hardt, Michael and Negri, Antonio (2000) *Empire*, Cambridge, MA: Harvard University Press.

Haskell, Molly (1974) *From Reverence to Rape: The Treatment of Women in the Movies*, Harmondsworth: Penguin Books.

Humphries, Reynold (1975) "*Numéro Deux*, Godard's Synthesis: Politics and the Personal," *Jump Cut* 9: 12–13.

Iser, Wolfgang (1978) *The Act of Reading: A Theory of Aesthetic Response*, Baltimore, MD: The Johns Hopkins University Press.

Jacobs, Lewis (1967) *The Rise of the American Film: A Critical History*, New York: Teachers College Press; first published in 1939.

James, David (1989) *Allegories of Cinema: American Film in the Sixties*, Princeton, NJ: Princeton University Press.

Jameson, Fredric (1991) *Postmodernism, Or the Cultural Logic of Late Capitalism*, Durham, NC: Duke University Press.

Jauss, Hans Robert (1982) *Toward an Aesthetic of Reception*, translation from the German by Timothy Bahti, introduction by Paul deMan, Minneapolis, MN: University of Minnesota Press.

Kawin, Bruce (1992) *How Movies Work*, Berkeley, CA: University of California Press.

Lacan, Jacques (1998) *On Feminine Sexuality: The Limits of Love and Knowledge*, translated with notes by Bruce Fink, New York: Norton.

Lane, Christina (2000) *Feminist Hollywood: From 'Born in Flames' to 'Point Break'*, Detroit, MI: Wayne State University Press.

Landy, Marcia (1991) *British Genres: Cinema and Society, 1930 –1960*, Princeton, NJ: Princeton University Press.

—— (1996) *Cinematic Uses of the Past*, Minneapolis, MN: University of Minnesota Press.

Leach, Jim (2004) *British Film*, Cambridge: Cambridge University Press.

Lindsay, Vachel (1970) *The Art of the Motion Picture*, with an introduction by Stanley Kauffmann, New York: Liveright Publishing Company; first published in 1915.

Lumet, Sidney (1995) *Making Movies*, New York: Vintage Books.

McCarthy, Anna (2001) *Ambient Television: Visual Culture and Public Space*, Durham, NC: Duke University Press.

Manovich, Lev (2001) *The Language of New Media*, Cambridge, MA: MIT Press.

Morley, David (1986) *Family Television: Cultural Power and Domestic Leisure*, London: Comedia Publishing Group.

Mulvey, Laura (1975) "Visual Pleasure and Narrative Cinema," *Screen* 16(3) (Autumn): 6–18.

——(1992) *Citizen Kane*, London: BFI Publishing.

——(2004) "Les Quatre Premiers Plans d'Imitation of Life," *Trafic* 10.

Okome, Onookome (2004) "Women, Religion, and the Video Film in Nigeria," *Film International* 7(1).

Penley, Constance (1997) *NASA / Trek*, London: Verso.

Prince, Stephen (1996) "True Lies: Perceptual Realism, Digital Images, and Film Theory," *Film Quarterly* 49(3).

Powdermaker, Hortense (1950) *Hollywood: The Dream Factory*, Boston, MA: Little, Brown.

Prasad, M. Madhava (1998) *Ideology of the Hindi Film: A Historical Construction*, Delhi and New York: Oxford University Press.

Radway, Janice (1984) *Reading the Romance: Women, Patriarchy, and Popular Literature*, Chapel Hill, NC: University of North Carolina Press.

Rajadhyaksha, Ashish and Willemen, Paul (1994) *Encyclopaedia of Indian Cinema*, Oxford and New Delhi: Oxford University Press and BFI Publishing.

Ramsey, Nancy (2005) "The Hidden Cost of Documentaries," *The New York Times* (October 16).

Renan, Sheldon (1967) *An Introduction to the American Underground Film*, New York: Dutton.

Risen, Clay (2005) "Collapsing the Distribution Window," *The New York Times* (December 11).

Rony, Fatimah Tobing (1996) *The Third Eye: Race, Cinema, and Ethnographic Spectacle*, Durham, NC: Duke University Press.

Ross, Lillian (2002) *Picture*, New York: DaCapo Press; first published in 1952.

Said, Edward (1978) *Orientalism*, New York: Pantheon Books.

Shohat, Ella and Stam, Robert (eds.) (1994) *Unthinking Euro-centrism: Multiculturalism and the Media*, London: Routledge.

Sklar, Robert (1993) *Film: An International History of the Medium*, Englewood Cliffs, NJ: Prentice Hall; New York: Harry N. Abrams.

Sobchack, Vivian (2004) *Carnal Thoughts: Embodiment and Moving Image Culture*, Berkeley, CA: University of California Press.

Solnit, Rebecca (2003) *River of Shadows: Eadweard Muybridge and the Technological Wild West*, New York: Viking Press.

Spivak, Gayatri (1987) "Scattered Speculations on the Question of Value," *In Other Worlds: Essays in Cultural Politics*, New York: Methuen.

Spoto, Donald (1984) *The Dark Side of Genius: The Life of Alfred Hitchcock*, New York: Ballantine Books.

Studlar, Gaylyn (1988) *In the Realm of Pleasure: Von Sternberg, Dietrich, and the Masochist Aesthetic*, Urbana, IL: University of Illinois Press.

Thompson, Anne (2005) "F / X Gods: The 10 Visual Effects Wizards who Rule Hollywood," *Wired Magazine* 13(2) (February).

Thompson, Emily (2002) *The Soundscape of Modernity: Architectural Acoustics and the Culture of Listening in America, 1900–1933*, Cambridge, MA: The MIT Press.

Thompson, Frank (1996) *Lost Films: Important Movies That Disappeared*, New York: Citadel Press.

Tinkcom, Matthew (2002) *Working Like a Homosexual: Camp, Capital, Cinema*, Durham, NC: Duke University Press.

Toulet, Emmanuelle (1995) *Birth of the Motion Picture*, New York: Harry N. Abrams; first published in 1988.

Williams, Alan (1992) *Republic of Images: A History of French Filmmaking*, Cambridge, MA: Harvard University Press.

Williams, Linda (1989) *Hardcore: Power, Pleasure and the "Frenzy of the Visible"*, Berkeley CA: University of California Press.

Williams, Raymond (1976) *Keywords: A Vocabulary of Culture and Society*, New York: Oxford University Press.

Wollen, Peter (1992) *Singin' in the Rain*, London: BFI Publishing.

Wyatt, Justin (1998) "The Formation of the 'Major Independent': Miramax, New Line and the New Hollywood," in Steve Neale and Murray Smith (eds.) *Contemporary Hollywood Cinema*, London: Routledge.

Yúdice, George (2003) *The Expediency of Culture: Uses of Culture in the Global Era*, Durham, NC: Duke University Press.

Zimmermann, Patricia R. (2000) *States of Emergency: Documentaries, Wars, Democracies*, Minneapolis, MN: University of Minnesota Press.

INDEX

Cinema Studies:
The Key Concepts

Susan Hayward

Ranging from Bollywood superstar Amitabh Bachchan to Quentin Tarantino, from auteur theory to the Hollywood blockbuster, *Cinema Studies: The Key Concepts* has firmly established itself as the essential guide for anyone interested in film.

Now fully revised and updated for its third edition, the book includes new topical entries such as:

- Action movies
- Art direction
- Blockbusters
- Bollywood
- Exploitation cinema
- Female masquerade

Providing accessible and authoritative coverage of a comprehensive range of genres, movements, theories and production terms, *Cinema Studies: The Key Concepts* is a must-have guide to a fascinating area of study and arguably the greatest art form of modern times.

0-415-36782-4

Available at all good bookshops
For ordering and further information please visit
www.routledge.com